Playing with Dynamite

SHARON HARRIGAN

Playing with Dynamite

A MEMOIR

Contemporary Nonfiction
Truman State University Press
Kirksville, Missouri

Copyright © 2017 Sharon Harrigan / Truman State University Press, Kirksville,
    Missouri, 63501
tsup.truman.edu

Second printing, March 2018

Cover design: Lisa Ahrens
All photographs from the author's private collection.

Library of Congress Cataloging-in-Publication Data

Names: Harrigan, Sharon, 1967– author.
Title: Playing with dynamite : a memoir / by Sharon Harrigan.
Description: Kirksville, Missouri : Truman State University Press, 2017. |
    Series: Contemporary nonfiction
Identifiers: LCCN 2017017003 | ISBN 9781612482101 (pbk. : alk. paper)
Subjects: LCSH: Harrigan, Sharon, 1967– | Fathers and daughters—United
    States—Biography. | Harrigan, Sharon, 1967—Family. | Fathers—Death.
Classification: LCC CT275.H385637 A3 2017 | DDC 306.874/2—dc23
LC record available at https://lccn.loc.gov/2017017003

To my brother, mother, aunt, and uncle—for sharing your memories with me.

And to my husband, James—for sharing everything.

"Family? Secrets? Sometimes I think they are the same thing."

—*Michael Hainey*

"[Writing] is a sustained act of empathy."

—*Andre Dubus III*

"I want my feet to be bare,
I want my face to be shaven and my heart—
you can't plan on the heart, but
the better part of it, my poetry, is open."

—*Frank O'Hara*

Note to readers: This book is not about what happened in my childhood. Instead, it is an account of what I remembered and why I remembered it that way. I know I do not have the complete story because the story will keep growing the more I talk to people about it. I have not falsified anything, beyond changing a few names to protect privacy and reordering a few events. But I know now, in a way I didn't before starting this book, that the truth is a moving target. This is a work of nonfiction. There are no composite characters. Some of the dialogue is the product of recorded interviews, some has been recreated from memory, and some came from my imagination. I have tried to be clear in the text which is which.

Prologue

Overleaf: My father and his Jeep, summer 1974

October 2013

"I ALWAYS HATED FATHER'S DAY. Did I need a holiday to remind me that I couldn't remember my father?" I leaned against a rickety white podium and read those lines.

A fire roared against my back. My audience—the two dozen or so writers, painters, and musicians I'd spent the past two weeks at an arts residency with—stopped jiggling their plastic cups or crossing their knees or listening to the faint moos and neighs from nearby farms.

By the end of my reading I remembered a lot. A group crowded around me, but not to ask questions. They didn't want to talk about my father or about the piece I had just read. They wanted to tell me about *their* fathers.

Later, a friend asked if I was disappointed that nobody had asked any questions. "No," I said. "If talking about my father makes people talk about theirs, that's the best response of all." One of the most powerful things that hearing other people's stories can do is connect us to our own.

When I stood at the podium that fall in front of my peers, I was a few weeks away from a fact-finding trip that would either confirm or destroy the stories I'd always told myself about my father. I wasn't sure if I had the courage to embark on that trip. I was jealous of my reputation as a good daughter, and keeping family stories secret seemed to be what good daughters did.

I lingered with my audience, eating pretzels and nuts and drinking wine. One woman, though, hovered in the back and slipped out early. Anaya was in her twenties and came from a traditional Indian American family, with whom she still lived, commuting to work from her childhood bedroom. During my reading, she'd crouched with her elbows knifing her knees, her face stretched with a deep emotion I couldn't read.

The next morning, she found me at breakfast and asked if we could sit alone at a table in the corner. She dug her serrated grapefruit knife into the fruit's soft flesh, and I imagined she was about to chastise me for being a bad daughter.

"I couldn't say this last night," she said. "I was too emotional. But I wanted to thank you for what you read. It felt like you were telling the story of *my* father."

Unlike mine, her father was still alive. He grew up in Delhi, not Detroit. He was an engineer, not a welder. In so many superficial ways, our fathers were nothing alike. But as she told me more about growing up with the man who defined her as a woman, I came to see that there is something primal about our relationships with our fathers, something deep and complicated we all share.

The story of my missing my father made her realize she'd been missing her own, even though she saw him every day. We left the table and wound our way up the path towards the farm buildings converted into writers' studios. I didn't yet know what her gratitude meant, but it fortified me for my journey.

Part 1
Stories We Tell

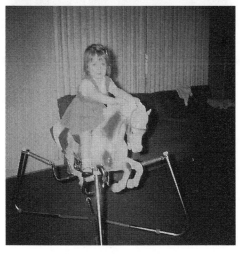

Overleaf: (*top*) Louis and his fish, July 1969; (*bottom*) Mr. Ed and me, October 1968

November 2013

W<small>HEN MY FATHER TOOK MY</small> six-year-old sister on a trip to kill a deer, the deer killed him. They were still winding their way Up North, driving the four-hour trip from suburban Detroit to the country. In the pre-dawn fog, a buck ran into the middle of the road, the soft-top Jeep crashed, turned upside down, and crushed my father. My sister survived, and my mother was left to care for three small, bewildered children on her own. My brother was nine, I was seven. My father was thirty-two, my mother twenty-nine. The year was 1974. This is our family story.

We tell ourselves stories in order to live, Joan Didion famously said. I've wrapped myself up in this story's shelter, the comfort of its familiarity which, after many repetitions, starts to feel the same as its truth.

I was home asleep, but I'd always imagined that night this way.

Like all Michigan Novembers, this one's cold. No snow, though. Not yet. At least Downstate. Likely my father will encounter flakes and flurries as his Jeep climbs up the middle of the mitten-shaped state, so he packs snow boots, ski masks, and a parka for my little sister, Lynn, her own tiny mittens clipped to the sleeves. He'll help her build the biggest snowman south of the Yukon before this trip is done, an Abominable Snowman, so she'll need an extra pair of mittens too for that. "Midge!" he yells, and my mother flies out of the house like a hound heeding a command. "Get me some waterproof ones," he says, and she does, her long blonde hair slapping against her cheek.

"I can't . . . ," she stammers and stops.

"What, woman? You can't finish a sentence?"

"This fog . . . ," she says, batting the thick mist away with her tiny hands.

"I can see fine," he says, his tone implying x-ray vision.

Soon she skitters back in, her thin skin shivering.

Before he packs his little girl he packs his gear: orange vests and stocking caps, a rifle in the front, coffee in a thermos near his feet, some clothes and food. Excalibur, the beagle we call Ex for short, jumps in the trunk, wagging his tail, slobbering on my father's only hand that loads sacks of apples and sugar beets for deer. Then Ex whinnies and wiggles, his body saying these road trips, these hunting treks, are what he lives for.

My father has grown a beard as red as his hair to insulate him from the elements. Truth is, though, no chill can penetrate him. If a bee stung, he wouldn't feel it. Frostbite? He'd bite right back. His Levis, marked from welding sparks, are all about work, like his tan suede boots. His psychedelic trucker cap is something else. Even though he exhales frost, sweat forms on his brow after he heaves bullets and belts to ride next to the dog. His right sleeve hangs hollow, flapping in the wind.

He loads my sister Lynn in back and tucks her in a green wool Army surplus blanket, lays her down across the bench seat, fluffs her pillow, tells her, "Go on, go to sleep." She sticks her thumb in her mouth only after he's no longer looking.

They drive up Fort Street, turn left at Southfield Road, passing dark alleys, empty lots, and graffitied storefronts: White Castle, Sam's Beer Store, and A&W Root Beer stand. Then my father tips his knees to steer the wheel (his left hand clutching coffee) to merge on I-75 North, speed limit 55. He's going 70. At least.

My father drives and drives, as the radio plays his favorite artists: Johnny Cash, Bob Dylan, Marty Robbins. The fog thickens. My sister sleeps and sleeps. The dog too, the engine hum the perfect white noise. The road slicks as the temperature drops each mile north they drive. My father quickens his pace, up to 80 now, maybe more. Hardly another car on the road. The sooner they arrive the sooner he can sleep himself.

Then, hours in, it happens. A great big buck, the biggest buck in the Midwest or maybe the world, bigger than a truck (in my childish imagination) runs across the road, materializing from the mist. The Jeep hits its heavy flesh, skids, topples over, and crushes my father. His head is smashed, blood gushes out his eyes. He cracks like an egg.

That's the story I tell myself about my father's death.

This is the story I tell myself about his life: He was a natural wonder. He lost his right, dominant hand and forearm before I was born, "playing with dynamite," but he could do more with one limb than everybody else could with two. When he wasn't balancing a stick of fire, melting metal to metal to make buildings and factories in Motor City (which I later learned was called welding), he was stalking game in the wild or inventing machines in a dungeon-like den carved out of the laundry room in our basement. There were probably dragons breathing fire to power his tools. He stockpiled gold leaf in there too, which he used for chemistry experiments, he said, but I was sure he'd turned lead to gold from alchemy. His legs were so long and strong, in one stride he could cover half the woods, so running with all the might of my little-kid legs I'd never catch him, then he'd lean back, sweep me onto his shoulders, and bark, "This is your last joyride, kid. Better toughen up." He could shoot deer and pheasants and rabbits, by the bucketful, when no one else could even track down an animal at all, the whole forest as barren as if an evil spell had been cast on it.

The story of my father's life doesn't square with the story of his death. He was the kind of man who killed animals, not the kind who could be killed by one.

This is the story my mother tells about me: I'm eighteen months old, springing up and down on the bouncy horse we call Mr. Ed while my mother rocks and nurses my newborn baby sister. I fall off and scrape my knees, dry eyed. "Don't worry, Mommy," I apparently say. "I can kiss my own boo-boos." Kiss, kiss. Then I climb back in the saddle.

We live in our stories, sometimes, because it's more comfortable than living in real life.

This is the story I tell myself about my brother: In elementary school and junior high, he teaches himself to read in English, German, and Latin. Instead of rocking to the Bee Gees and leafing through Archie comic books, he belts along with Wagner's five-hour operas on his yellow, plastic turntable and writes a dissertation proving to his seventh grade English teacher that Francis Bacon wrote Shakespeare's plays. Why? Where does Louis get these crazy ideas? Not from the neighborhood kids playing freeze tag and capture the flag. Maybe he fell from the sky.

This is the story I tell myself about my sister: Hands calloused from the monkey bars, knees scraped from kneeling on concrete in the driveway while our father taught her to change the oil and make an engine purr, at six she is already a tomboy when my father tucks her into the backseat of the Jeep to hunt. It's too dark to drive, the air too thick, the road too slick, but physical obstacles were his specialty. My sister somehow survives, with a few scrapes on her knees, no worse than mine from Mr. Ed. But she can't kiss her own boo-boos, not the ones on the inside, anyway. As she grows up, lifting weights, hiking mountains, and fixing cars, something stays broken.

This is the story I tell myself about my mother: Be careful or you'll lose her too. When one person dies, another will soon. Maybe if I don't upset her, she'll stay safe. Above all, don't talk about what happened to my father.

The story I tell about myself is this: I'm a phony. I live in a college town, I'm married to a professor, and I'm surrounded by academics and intellectuals. I pretend to be one of them, but my brain is stuck in a mythical land where deer attack, and they win, in a kind of poetic justice I'll call Revenge of the Prey. I am my father's daughter. I can't know anything about myself unless I first find out about him.

But deep down in the magical thinking of the seven-year-old I was when I learned that death is real, using the kind of fairy-tale logic that imprinted in my brain even as I grew and aged and birthed my own children, I was so convinced my whole life, without forming the thought in words, that asking about my father might kill me.

Why did I think that? I couldn't say. But I hoped—and dreaded—I'd soon find out.

An hour earlier, I'd flown into Detroit Metro, where my aunt and uncle met me at Arrivals and ferried me back to their house. Now I sank into the soft plush of their couch, a gas fire licking in the hearth, and ferreted a phone from my front jeans pocket. My uncle passed me a bowl of Halloween-size chocolate treats, and my aunt offered coffee. I emptied my cup, though I didn't need my heart sped up. I would have traded half my left pinkie for a beer, if I hadn't been too shy to ask. "Mind if I record?"

"Go right ahead," my uncle said.

I turned the tape recorder on.

April 2011

LEAVE ME THERE IN MICHIGAN, for now, shivering with something other than cold as my aunt fetches a blanket and covers my knees. Let me dangle for a while before asking the questions I'd spent two and a half years preparing for. Keep the recorder on my phone running in the background as it collects hours and hours of talk over many days and miles.

Rewind with me to the brink of my fact-finding journey. Springtime in Virginia. Classical columns on campus and lining the streets, in the city Thomas Jefferson modeled on ancient Greece.

Dogwoods and azaleas at their peak, covering our shoes with pink and white. Trees filled with birdsong.

We tell our children stories so they won't whine that their little legs are too tired or beg to be carried. My third-grade daughter Ella and I were walking to school, and a story would distract her from the climb. Her long blonde braid, brightly flowered peasant skirt, and long, slim legs made her look like a miniature hippie or a Heidi doll. "Tell me again about the Cyclops," Ella begged. "Tell me about the Sirens."

We'd started reading *The Odyssey* early, a children's version, full of illustrations. I read it to Ella at bedtime, on the subway when we lived in New York City, and then, in the quiet Virginia college town we'd moved to, I retold the stories on our daily walks to elementary school.

My brother used to read *The Odyssey* to me. On the way to junior high, he splayed the yellowed paperback before his face, and his eyes never strayed from the page, even when he crossed the street and tipped an errant cart at A&P.

My husband, James, was in Paris, presenting a seminar on international trade to fellow economists, and in every e-mail he addressed me as "patient Penelope" and signed "your Odysseus."

Ella and I reached the top of St. Clair Avenue then turned right at Mowbray, her school finally in sight and Odysseus once again safe. "Now tell me how he escaped Scylla and Charybdis," she said. We sat on a bench and waited in the playground for the doors to open. "Tell me about the cows of Helios." While other children swung on swings and hung from jungle gyms, she leaned close to my ear and said, "Tell me about Calypso." And so I did.

At home, I found the grown-up version. It doesn't start with monsters or goddesses or even Odysseus. First is the Telemachiad, the search of Telemachus for his father, missing twenty years. The story of a son who can't remember his father. Of someone who only knows his heritage through hearsay.

Patient? I'm not Penelope at all. Not the waiting woman but the searching son.

As the epic opens, Telemachus sets sail to interview those who might tell him what befell his father. He's heard rumors, fragments, speculation. Athena, in disguise, goads him to outfit a ship and seek what news he can in the islands beyond Ithaca. Only then will he be man enough to oust all uninvited visitors, to seize control of his ancestral home.

Athena didn't urge me on, so I was older than twenty when I began my own Telemachiad. I was in my forties, and what spurred me to action was my son.

ONE SATURDAY AFTERNOON I CARRIED a trunkful of food into my kitchen from the organic butcher, Asian grocery, fish store, and supermarket. Four different stops to shop for a few days of overly complicated recipes. Why? Good question. When James asked, I replied, "Because I have time."

Before this second marriage, I was a single mother working as a textbook and research journals managing editor in the day and freelancing at night, after I tucked in my son. I was saving up to move to a quieter, safer Brooklyn apartment.

Now, editing part time and writing magazine features on such elevated topics as "teaching your teen to drive" (as if I knew) left me more time than I'd ever had.

Since I was fourteen, I'd always worked, often as much as twenty hours a week even during school months. At A&W, Dairy Queen, KFC, and a title insurance agency in high school. At law firms and hospitals during college. Now that James had tenure and we'd sold our house in Brooklyn for more than twice what houses cost here, we could manage without two full salaries.

At least, to earn my keep, I could try to satisfy my husband's every whim. I wasn't aware of that intention at the time. "I could ask you to do anything, and you would," James said to me at least once a week when he saw that I'd turned, say, his comment about how much he liked home-grown tomatoes into the neighborhood's most impressive backyard garden. "It would be so easy to take advantage of you," he said. "I have to be careful."

I had to be careful too. No matter how long I knew James, even after we married, co-signed mortgages, and had a child together, I still worried he'd see through me. I learned to buy the most artisanal baby vegetables, light candles on the dining room table, and even pretend to be a fellow food snob. But when James was away—collecting data or delivering seminar papers—the kids and I sometimes tore into burgers in front of the TV or scooped out Chinese food with plastic forks. Each time he traveled my disguise fell away. It would be so easy to forget to put it back on.

James had mentioned in passing that week how much he missed the Japanese noodle restaurants near his old office in Manhattan, so I shopped for all the esoteric ingredients. I wore a green wool sweater to cover the thin skin I'd inherited from my always-cold mother ("redheads should wear green," everyone said, and who was I not to listen?) and ankle boots even though this spring was warm and lush, the landscape yellowed and pinked with pollen and blossoms.

The only person home when I returned from shopping was my sixteen-year-old son Noah. I stood on a stepstool and unloaded my groceries, while he hovered over the stove—long black sideburns, thick black hair, his body dwarfing mine—and stirred a pot of tortellini for lunch. The last line of his T-shirt read, "Haikus are easy / But sometimes they don't make sense / Refrigerator."

Noah turned on the timer for the pasta, poured himself a glass of milk, then asked, "Want some?"

"No thanks." I plucked a bottle of *nam pla* from a pink breast cancer awareness sack and placed it on the pantry shelf. "Do you know what day it is?"

"Tax day?"

"It's also your dad's birthday."

"I *know*," he said. Of course he did.

"Are you going to e-mail him?"

Noah shrugged.

"Maybe send an e-card?"

When Noah was nine, his father, my ex-husband Andrew, tried to kill himself by overdosing on prescription tranquilizers. He didn't die, but something changed after that.

"I don't want to have this conversation," Noah said.

"Me neither."

"Then why'd you bring it up?"

I unloaded bag after bag in silence. Beef marrow bones and panko, lemongrass and ginger. Noah stirred and stirred, scraping the pot so hard I thought he'd dig a hole in the bottom.

"He keeps contacting me," I finally said. "Says you don't return his e-mails or phone calls."

"And your point is?"

"I just told him we'd talk about it."

"I'd rather not."

"But . . ."

"You want to talk about *your* dad?" Noah asked me.

I stopped rustling the bags to hear better. My dad? What did he have to do with it? "No."

"I thought so." He turned toward me for the first time, his lips scrunched into something like a conspiratorial grin.

I dropped a bag of potatoes on my foot, then cried out more loudly than a bag of potatoes should warrant. Maybe I was showing Noah how children could forget their fathers.

The timer dinged, Noah drained the tortellini, poured it in a bowl, and carried it across the threshold to the basement, where he slouched down to his bedroom.

Maybe children who learned to ignore their fathers could even, someday, ignore their mothers. Noah's Xbox fired up with a swoosh, as he started Call of Duty.

I HADN'T TALKED ABOUT MY father in years. Noah was trying to tell me something. Children can pick up on what we *don't* say, can't they?

Not long after Andrew's birthday came Ella's. She turned eight.

I woke with the sharp stab of a dream: I'm an actor in a play and forget my lines. All that changes each time is the script; that morning I was the *Alice in Wonderland* rabbit. "I'm late, I'm late." That's all dream-me remembered.

Over muesli and yogurt we shared the *New York Times*. Ella read James and me a story about migrating turtles, then I slipped out to water my garden, sprouts of mesclun and spinach in neat little rows and trellises for peas. Almost hidden behind an apple tree, two deer stood still and watched, so big my heart beat fast. I'd never lived before where deer ran free like squirrels. These grazed my lawn as if I'd planted it for them. They looked down at me.

They're not bears, I reminded myself. They're not magic. Not gods come to earth seeking vengeance. I didn't need to flee.

THE DEER IS A SYMBOL of goodness. He destroys evil. At least in the Middle Ages.

Medieval bestiaries show the deer, or stag, as Christ, hunting down the devil, in the form of a snake, pursuing the creature into a hole and then flushing it out by flooding the hole with water from its mouth. Finally, the deer devours its prey.

The snake's fangs and venom can poison, its coils can squeeze and suffocate. But the deer only has water. And supernatural power.

NOAH SLEPT IN, AND ELLA left for swim team carpool. James read me an article about the release of Guantanamo papers that showed a Saudi man leashed like a dog and forced to urinate on himself. Then we rode our bikes to yoga, single file.

In the afternoon, children arrived for Ella's party, half boys, half girls, and the economics graduate student we'd hired to dress up as a clown and twist balloons. He didn't just create poodles and swords. He rose to the challenge of each kid's request as if he were giving a dissertation defense. "You want a space ship? A rocket? You want a planet for it to land on? You want a tree on the planet? What else?"

We offered rubber ducky party favors, and the boys turned them into soldiers. The girls rebelled, using their balloons as peace protest signs. Finally, Ella opened her presents. Bookstore gift cards. Dime store jewelry. And a snow globe.

I had a snow globe when I was a little girl. I would stare into that glittery ball every night from my bed, and it helped me drift off into sleep, the swirling of the snow pacifying my mind and creating sweet dreams with its liquid motion. But it broke into tiny shards. How did that happen?

Then I remembered.

MY CHILDREN'S MILESTONES HELPED ME recover my own. I'd forgotten so much, just as in my dreams.

I don't know what compelled me to write about my father for the first time, or rather, what allowed me to remember him. Maybe the snow globe or the water in it. The white grit. The snowman. The visitation of winter in spring. Maybe the broken glass I could almost feel again, sharp on bare soles, scattered across my bedroom floor. Noah's words echoed in my head: "You want to talk about *your* father?"

Not long after that, I wrote these words on my blog, Walking on the Highway:

> Eight years ago today, sharp pains woke me in my hospital bed at 3:00 a.m. The doctor said, "Call your husband and tell him the baby will be born in 30 minutes." James arrived in 25, just as Ella's head poked out.

Ella is now older than I was when my father died, so if I die she will remember me better than I remember him. It's a morbid thought to have on a day of birth. I wonder if other people who've experienced death at a young age think this way too.

As a child, I kept expecting more people to die. This is what grown-ups did, right? I wondered—with a regularity that now seems neurotic—who would take care of my brother, sister, and me once my mother was gone.

Ella will never meet my father, who shared my red hair, liberal leanings, and rebel spirit. He will never take her hunting in the woods of northern Michigan, never teach her how to weld or navigate by the stars. He never did these things for me either, but I like to imagine he would have.

My father favored tomboys like my sister, and Ella is a girly-girl, but he would have loved her anyway. He would have taught her to make white bean soup and grilled cheese sandwiches the way he taught me. He would have taken her for walks in the forest, expecting her to keep up with his pace, four steps for every one of his.

He would have inspected her room for cleanliness, breaking her snow globes. He would have made her eat all the fat and gristle on her plate. He would have tolerated no crying ever ("You want me to give you something to cry about?"), but especially not on the happy day when Ella turned eight.

My brother read my blog post the day it appeared and e-mailed me right away. He said, "You remember our dad a lot better than I do."

Louis is a year and a half older than I am, and I'd always assumed he knew much more than I did. Not just about my father.

I wrote that to my brother, and he replied, "I've tried not to remember too much. So many of my memories are of Dad humiliating me in front of others. I still cry today when I think about some of the things he did to me. I wish I had felt close to him as you did—maybe I'd remember more." And then came the words I couldn't get out of my mind: "I was relieved when he died. It's terrible to say, but it's true."

This is the story I always told about my brother, sister, mother, and me: We shared a central tragedy, our father's death. People aren't relieved when a tragedy occurs. No matter what he did to us, he was our father, and losing a parent young is practically the definition of misfortune. What could Louis mean?

I could recall only a sliver, and that a blur of what I'd seen, been told, or guessed. A Mad Libs game of blanks I might have filled in wrong. But it was a start.

"Ella's turning eight makes me remember being eight," I wrote to Louis.

"I know," he said. "That's why I don't have kids."

When I tell people, especially parents of young children, that I don't remember much about my father, they don't want to believe me. Won't their children remember every moment of their time together? They've often given up jobs, friends, hobbies, passions, even sex lives in exchange for memory-making moments. It's an investment they want to pay off.

Was it true I couldn't remember? Or that I wouldn't? If I wanted to know what Louis meant, I had to try.

Perhaps I should reassure my friends, telling them their children won't need to block out memories. Won't need to do what I was just starting to realize I had done all my life.

Memories of watching my father drive for hours on the highway, steering only with his knees, as I braced for a crash. Shielding my eyes as he punished our puppy by throwing him in the street. Swallowing the spoonfuls of whisky that burned our throats because he thought it would toughen us up. Hearing him tell everyone he would take our little sister hunting instead of my older brother, because she was more of a man than Louis would ever be.

These were moments I wasn't sure I wanted to remember.

I DIDN'T HAVE A CHOICE. My blog and e-mails with my brother opened a Pandora's box. I could no longer keep my childhood locked inside.

In one of my first memories, I'm three or four, and Lou is five or six. Lynn is still a toddler, in her crib asleep. Dinner done, we hover on the scratchy shag outside our parents' door. Louis reads a picture book to me, about a puppy that digs under the fence. I hold the current *Playboy* in my hands and flip through the cartoons. I grabbed it from the coffee table, in plain sight. I don't need to read to know these pictures are funny. Just look at the shapes of all these bulges and bellies, how ridiculous our bodies are. Breasts I know; I've seen my mother nurse my sister. But the cartoon breasts are birthday party helium balloons. I want one on a string. They make me laugh.

Lou can read. He's magic to me, and I will never catch up. But he's so grown up he's tired of all his tricks and pretends to be a baby. "Ga ga goo goo," he says. "Me want milkie."

"Me want berry." I pretend to eat the fruit printed on my pajamas.

We listen to the squeal of the springs, the bouncing up and down. And then a cry. Is someone hurt? So much we don't yet understand. Only now do I see that those squeaks and cries were sounds, not of pain, but love.

In my memory, my parents "jump on the bed" every night after dishes are cleared, but that can't be right. Just as Noah now will say that "every day" I was late to pick him up from after school, from kindergarten till fifth grade, but maybe I missed the train and left him waiting twice a year. When an event is intense, it can seem continuous.

THE NEXT BLOCKED OUT MEMORY was this: I'm six and my father brings home a tiny two-month-old puppy. He's even cuter than in the picture books—white and brown and black, a big wet nose, ears that flop, a tail set on perpetual wag. He's so small that even I can be tougher than him. He's a baby, and I want to scoop him up and rock him like my baby doll.

We're in our backyard, bruised apples littered on the ground from our tree, the chain fence missing a few links, an empty lot turned pipeline our view. Ex is so minuscule he slips right under the sharp tines of the metal and scampers into the street. My father runs and sweeps him in his arm. But then he drops him. No, throws him. "You like the street?" he asks our dog. "I'll give you the street." Splat. I shield my eyes but still hear the sound.

"You shouldn't do that to our dog," my mother says, after our father ties him to his doghouse.

"Not *our* dog," my father says. "He's *mine.*"

THIS ONE MY BROTHER CAN'T recall. Our family readies for a trip Up North, starting, as usual, at four in the morning. We scurry to dress and pack, even in our semi-sleepwalk state, our pulses quickening with thoughts of scampering free in the woods and purpling our mouths with ripe, wild berries. Then we see our father knocked back out on the couch. "Daddy, aren't we going?" I ask, hovering close to his snore. He wakes up with a start and yells, "Now we're not." The paneling almost falls off the walls when his fist hits the coffee table.

"Why?"

"Blame your sister," he tells my siblings, "for bothering me." After that, I stay out of his way.

I'M EIGHT YEARS OLD, BELLY down on the shag, soles in the air, chin propped on hands, elbows grinding into the carpet. I'm as close as I can get to the TV, my routine for Saturday morning, the best time of the week. My favorite show comes on. My hero is all action, like a silent movie star. No need to talk, and yet today he says, "I am Wile E. Coyote, Super Genius." His accent, a little British, a little academic, a little royal, is, to me, the sound of intelligence.

THEN CAME MEMORIES OF STORIES I'd heard, of things I hadn't witnessed myself. I wasn't born when my parents met, but my imagined version goes this way.

She's sixteen, her waist-length hair in a blonde ponytail, the brown-and-orange miniskirt of her A&W uniform swinging with her slight hips, white Keds slapping the asphalt. She delivers a plastic tray of two frothy mugs and a pair of footlongs to the red Chevy parked in #17.

It's my father's car. His brother Barry sits in the passenger seat. She's small but beautiful.

He's nineteen, his red hair and mustache so bright she can't help staring. Plus, there's something about the way he looks at her, something so strong, masculine, and intense about his gaze, like the look I've stared at in his wedding photo. She's not usually caught off balance when men take notice of her, but this time she knocks his mug of root beer over as she snaps the tray to his window.

"Sorry," she says. Her voice is soft and sweet, a voice that makes it difficult for me to hear her on the phone even now.

"Don't worry," he says. "I'll give you another chance. Here tomorrow?"

She is. After school every weekday till 11 p.m. He returns by himself but orders two mugs. "One's for you," he says when she delivers his tray. "Mind if I buy you a drink?"

How can she resist? Out of all the other carhops he'd picked her at first sight. He is so sure, he makes her confident too. His long-sleeved shirt covers his stump, and she doesn't yet know his right hand is missing. It's the left one she notices, the calluses of a man who knows a hard day's work. She likes that.

Isn't it romantic? Think Clint Eastwood. Steve McQueen.

I can picture every crooked scratch on the refrigerator door at the A&W branch on Southfield Road where my mother worked. I can still smell the stale oil in the deep fryers and see the grease on chili dogs. Because I worked there too.

Why? Was I hoping, at fourteen, to meet my own future husband? Did I scan the cars every shift, choose the customer I wanted, spill root beer on him, and see if it had the same effect it had on my father?

I can list many reasons I took that job. It was the only place I knew that hired such young girls. The pay was 50 percent more than the going rate for teenage babysitters. The logic is plausible. But beyond those surface justifications, in a place buried deep in the magical thinking of my child brain, lurks something more murky and compelling.

Only now can I see why I worked where my parents met. If my father returned, that's where I thought he'd appear.

Yet I couldn't forget what my brother had said: "I was relieved when he died. It's terrible to say, but it's true." What had my father done? I let myself remember.

EVERY WEEK, BEFORE PARCELING OUT the grocery money, he'd ask my mother to weigh herself. I listened in my bedroom to the creak and whine of the bathroom scale, hoping she'd remembered to pee, wondering if each extra ounce would mean less money for our lunches, only peanut butter and no jelly for our sandwiches. Bologna but no mayonnaise. Maybe this week, enough for chocolate chip cookies?

Instead of eating lunch, she drank her stingy allotment of "Liquid Protein." It was as red as Faygo Redpop but smelled like blue toilet bowl cleaner. White plastic bottles lined our cabinets, and when she unscrewed one of the tops the whole kitchen fumed.

In the morning, with no solid food in her belly, she turned on the daily exercise show. Jack LaLanne, with his peppy voice and his even peppier wife Elaine LaLanne, the woman with the tongue-twister name, cheered my mother on in her quest to make part of herself disappear.

She did sit-up after sit-up and stood on her head while we toddlers and preschoolers sat around and watched. When Jack asked for a squat, she turned it into a duck waddle. "Come on, baby ducks!" she cheered us on to follow her, up and down the narrow hall. "Now reverse, baby ducks! Waddle, waddle, waddle, and I'll follow, follow, follow. Then we'll plop into the pond." As soon as we reached the living room we dove into the couch. "Plop!" my mother said. Then my brother said "Ploop!" I said "Poop!" and my sister screamed "Poopy!" We all squealed in delight.

"No poop jokes, ducklings!" my mother said.

"Squat, squat, squat!" shouted Jack LaLanne. "Get rid of that fat!"

"Waddle, waddle, waddle," my mother said, and we mimicked her. "Shake those duckie butts."

"Duck food!" we begged.

"Not yet!" my mother said. "Shake, shake, shake."

"Chocolate shake! Ice cream!" We rolled over in giggles while our mother did jumping jacks past our capacity to count them, then sweated and jumped and stretched while we collapsed in a puddle.

One day at lunchtime, I was inspired by the Three Stooges to throw an open peanut butter sandwich in my sister's face, coconut-cream-pie style. Lynn cried. No TV laugh track told me I was funny.

I still had to eat it. "It's got Lynn's face on it. She cried all over it. It's got her snot."

But I couldn't waste good food. I had to remember all the hungry people.

I thought she meant oceans away. Not in the next seat, sliding me my plate.

I watched Road Runner cartoons on TV, over and over. Behind a boulder Coyote huddles, spying his prey. "Meep! Meep!" Road Runner beeps. Coyote casts a fishing pole, dynamite tied to the end, aiming for the bird. The stick hits its target, bounces, then lands in a crater filled with a rock as big as a truck. Boom! The rock pops up and boomerangs. Coyote, left holding the fishing line, is crushed.

But he rises again. He always tries again. A rocket on his back explodes. Then he digs a hole, fills it with dynamite, and covers it

with a tarp. Yards away, he lights the long fuse. Meep! Meep! Road
Runner taunts him, and Coyote grabs the bait, chasing till he falls
in his own trap and blows up.

And is resurrected.

Every time, my heart pumps fast. Every time I cheer him; "Go
on. Catch your prey."

Wile E. Coyote is a hunter. A lover of gadgets. He probably
tinkers with inventions in a den carved out of the laundry room in
his basement, I think, as a little kid. I bet he drives with his knees.
Likely, dragons breathe fire to power his tools. He doesn't catch the
bird, but I don't care. Every few minutes he blows up then wipes the
soot and ashes from his fur and schemes again. The screen fades to
black, but he always comes back.

I thought my father might return too.

MY MOTHER WAS NEVER HANDY. I'm not either, but in her day, it
wasn't ladylike to learn how to unclog a drain, to jiggle the nozzle
of a recalcitrant furnace to fire it up, to replace crumbling tiles in
the shower.

People must have said we should have moved to an apartment
and let the landlord fix everything that was broken. But perhaps my
mother heard, as we did as kids, something strange in the cracks
and the creaks and the drip, drip, dripping leaks. We wouldn't have
called it a ghost. We wouldn't have spoken about it at all.

My father worked too many jobs all his life to fix our faucets
and floors. He meant to, but never had time. What else did he have
now? A whole eternity.

I SEARCHED FOR MEMORIES I'D left on the highway too.

I'm five years old, and I open my eyes after sleeping from four
to seven, the rosy fingers of Dawn, as Homer says, lifting over the
horizon. My stomach lurches as we swoosh down a hill, my little
sister laughing, my mother shielding her eyes so she can't see my

father lifting his only hand in the air, showing he can steer with his hips and his legs or maybe just by the power of will. She mumbles, maybe a prayer; it's a low rumble impossible to decipher, a kind of white noise. My big brother lets out a high-pitched gasp; he's old enough and smart enough to anticipate the consequences of a vehicle stopping and skidding on a dime. "Come on, be a man," is my father's response. We hit the bottom of the hill. My sister begs my father, "Do it again!"

I don't like to recall my father teaching my mother to drive. I'm about five. We three kids lean on each other's shoulders in the back bench seat of our dark blue Pontiac. I cradle my baby doll, the one with the yellow nightgown and the eyes that close when you lay her down to sleep and open when you sit her upright. Lynn clutches a tiny T. rex, and Louis spreads something to read on his lap. My mother's in the driver's seat, my father's riding shotgun. "Now Midge, that was a dumb ass thing to do," he says. I don't know what she did that time. Yield when she had the right of way? Brake too jerky? Accelerate in starts and stops? Not check her mirrors? She does all these things, and each time he curses then he strikes her, or maybe he stabs his left elbow into her right rib, her side, her stomach. I don't want to look. I don't want to hear. I want to remember the lessons differently. I don't want to remember that the next day, it's sweltering and she wears a turtleneck. We don't ask why.

THAT JUNE, NOAH WAS LEARNING to drive. He'd finished Drivers Ed in school, passed the written test, and earned his permit. He had to log forty practice hours with a licensed driver, at least fifteen after dark.

At Noah's age, I didn't drive. I learned in Brooklyn in my twenties. Carrying Noah's stroller up and down the subway stairs provided ample motivation. I failed my first two road tests.

James worked long hours on research. He had ambitious plans for a sabbatical and teaching position in France, so he went to the office even on Sundays and holidays. Unlike him, I had time to teach my son. At every turn of the wheel, though, I gasped. Every time he hit the gas or brakes I braced for a crash. And driving at night? In New York City the bright lights illuminated every inch of the road, but here, the dark was too dark. Animals jumped out of the woods around every corner in Virginia, didn't they? Those deer that nibbled my grass in the morning had to go somewhere afterhours. I could drive at night myself, but teaching my son felt like risking our lives.

I tried not to ask James for help, but I had to. James is the one who taught Noah to drive. One night in June, after I tucked Ella in bed, James and Noah left to practice merging in the dark.

The only one awake in our silent house, the June light long but finally gone, I stared at my computer screen, trying to e-mail my brother. Why did he say he was relieved? Maybe he remembered those times in the back seat of the Pontiac. He might feel them in the ribs every time he took the wheel too. He might dread this time of year as much as I did. He might understand.

My breath came short and quick. My heart ticked at a clip almost as quick as my fingers. I'd won the typing award every year in high school and was so fast in college I snagged temp jobs making three times work-study pay.

"I always hated Father's Day," I typed, starting an e-mail to Louis. "Did I need a holiday to remind me that I couldn't remember my father?"

I didn't send the message. Instead, I turned it into an essay, incorporating my blog post, Louis's response, and all the memories of our childhood that had started flooding back through our conversations. Before James and Noah returned from their drive, I impulsively sent out the essay to a couple online magazines. I didn't think it would be accepted, so I didn't worry about hurting anyone's feelings. I called the piece "Revenge of the Prey: How a Deer Killed My Dad."

The next day, an online magazine called *The Rumpus* responded. My essay would appear that week, on Father's Day.

I was naive. I crossed my fingers, held my breath, and hoped that yanking my father back to the surface would cause no ripples. I didn't check with my mother to see if my facts were correct. I didn't ask her permission to share scenes intimate and sensitive, from her life, not just mine. I didn't ask my brother if I could tell the world he was glad his father was dead.

I was rushed. That's the story I told myself.

YOU'RE SWERVING ON BLACK ICE or falling down the stairs. A shadowy figure lurks in the alley waiting for you. An envelope bursts with promise for as long as you don't open it. That familiar prickle of a before-and-after moment told me something was about to change.

How many of us have experienced a fissure, a continental drift turning our lives into Part One and Part Two, creating a hole in the middle so big we don't dare look back and fall in? My father's death was that event for me. I hadn't turned around in decades. How bad could the consequences be?

I sent Louis the link to my Father's Day essay. Days went by. Finally, he responded, "I am sobbing like a five-year-old."

I dropped my head in my hands and bawled too. What had I done to him?

I MANAGED TO LOOK UP at my computer screen again. I'd read the tears wrong. The rest of the message said, "Thank you for the generosity and love that come through in your words. For helping me unbury some of those memories. You have given me back something valuable that I lost."

I called Louis in Austin. We told each other stories.

ON THE PHONE, WE ARE kids again, hovering outside our parents' room after dinner, baby-talking to each other to cover the sounds from inside.

On the phone, we are once again angsty teenagers, riding the bus downtown, then the Woodward Avenue transfer to the Detroit Institute of Arts in the depressed but arty neighborhood of the Cass Corridor to attend poetry classes and readings and watch art films that would never play in our blue-collar neighborhood. He reads aloud on the bus from the library books he picked out for me. Dostoyevsky. Marquez. Hesse. We pass the Pink Pussycat, its front window covered with a trash bag; the plasma donation center, advertising rates for donors; the empty nine-floor Hudson's department store, now a hollow shell; the abandoned Fox Theater, once a glamorous spot for live performances but now pimpled with graffiti; a dribble of men on corners talking into payphones, packing pistols. We are the only white people on the bus.

We're fourteen and fifteen, strolling through the art museum after poetry class in the afternoon, Louis, an art historian in the making, lecturing me on the Diego Rivera murals and the Albrecht engravings. Sometimes it seems as if we live in this building, we spend so much time in its marble halls, taking advantage of its policy of optional donation at the door. We stay for a film at night, Francois Truffaut's *The Green Room*. After the opening credits, a journalist mourns the death of his young wife and gathers her belongings into one green room then fills every inch with votive candles. The room burns down, so he finds a chapel in a church and consecrates it to his departed love. The lighting is creepy, the music macabre, the sound of the flickering flames a repetitive irritant. But we eat it up like candy. We cry and we watch each other cry, and we match our rhythms, silent and still, as only siblings can. Yet I'm aware, as we leave, strangers must think he's my boyfriend.

On the phone, again Louis becomes the prodigy who skipped eighth grade then moved to college after tenth, some of his high school classmates teasing him when he paints his nails black and starts listening to techno.

On the phone, again my sister is a teenage hundred-pound body-builder. On the front lawn of junior high, she fights a girl for calling her a profane name for fatherless child. A crowd gathers, cheering, as Lynn pummels the kid, who seems almost twice her weight, to the ground, and kicks her chin with the toe of her combat boot.

On the phone, again I am fourteen or fifteen, a waifish poet with a weird accent. Maybe I'm unconsciously imitating the Monty Python episodes I watch on PBS with Louis on his thirteen-inch black and white. I think I'm just enunciating clearly.

"Are you from England or something? Canada? You're not from around here, are you?" strangers ask.

You've probably never heard of my country, I should say. It's somewhere on the border of Earth and elsewhere. You have to be at least a half-orphan to get there. It's the place we go to meet our fathers.

IN THE DAYS AND MONTHS after I opened the Pandora's box containing our father, Louis visited me in Charlottesville for the first time. We e-mailed and phoned, sharing memories that weren't always the same.

We relived our father driving us to flea markets, scouring for odd tools and car parts in the hot sun. Taking Ex out to Ortonville to chase rabbits and flush out game birds, while we kids counted the tines of the railroad tracks. I told my brother how much I had wondered if "a hundred" and "one hundred" were separate numbers. How even as a little girl I sensed that others carried questions in their heads they wouldn't dare ask, things they never said so no one would know they didn't already know.

Louis didn't recall our father telling our mother she couldn't use a playpen. "Kids have to get hurt to learn," he told her.

He didn't remember our father asking us, as toddlers, "You want to go for a walk in the forest in the middle of the night? Jump on my shoulders. You want to learn to use a gun? Give it a try." The rifle weighed as much as we did.

When our father drove out into the Michigan countryside, he yanked us away from the toys he judged too tame and said, "You want to light a fire, crawl under a car, or cut open a rabbit? Don't listen to your ma or grandma. They'd never let you do anything. Just come with me." If Louis didn't remember these things, did I make them up?

TWO MEMORIES MY BROTHER HADN'T blocked out: our father teaching him German and our father humiliating him in public. I don't exactly remember these events myself, but I imagine them this way.

My father takes Louis to his den, a cubby of a crawl space inside the basement laundry room. It smells of mold and hibernating bears in there. A thousand drawers hold secret ingredients, small filaments and metals filings, metallic dust and strings and glass blown so thin it almost doesn't exist. This hermit space is off-limits to us kids alone, but sometimes our father invites one of us in. Usually not me. From this room my father plucks the books he gives us to read, dusty from the dirty floor. He slides a German grammar from the shelf. "*Ich* means I," he tells my brother. "Say that with your whole throat. It's guttural." Then maybe Louis says it well and earns a slap on the back. Maybe when he fails he has to dodge a stab in the rib.

The bullying is murky in my memory too. I've blocked it out. I can imagine my father, on the night he died, telling Lou, "What kind of sissy are you? Drawing pretty pictures in a notebook, while your baby sister's climbing trees? She's the son you will never be. I've a mind to take her hunting and leave you with the womenfolk." But I'd rather conjure a voice that sounded affectionate and teasing, instead of mean. I'd rather guess that my father chose my sister simply because she was the one who most wanted to go.

When my sister was suspended at school for bad-mouthing a teacher, instigating a fist fight, or smoking in the bathroom, the principal blamed our father's death. When Louis was denied a scholarship at an elite boarding school for "psychological reasons" even though he scored the highest on the entrance exam, our father's death was the culprit. (But recently, my mother added, "I think they said that to cover themselves. The real reason they didn't let him in was we were too poor.") I blamed my early bad choices in men on my father's death too.

I had resisted identifying with my brother, of thinking of myself as a potential victim. I wanted to be Coyote, not Roadrunner. I needed to stop telling myself that Louis was just the kind of kid who got teased.

We tell ourselves stories, sometimes, at the expense of others.

"I'm sorry," I said at the end of one of my phone conversations with Louis. I could hear, in the quiet that matched the ins and outs of my own breath (our sibling sounds), my brother crying too.

A FEW MONTHS AFTER I published "Revenge of the Prey," my mother flew in for Halloween.

One morning, my mother and I stood in my kitchen alone, washing breakfast dishes and pots I'd used for the Indian lentil stew I packed for James's lunch. ("Interesting," my mother called the menu, which I always translate as "weird.") Groundhogs scurried beyond the glass door, our backyard menagerie still such a novelty. Rabbits and hawks, skunks and opossums, the occasional fox and deer. More animals than in Brooklyn, where we'd recently lived, but also— strangely—more than in northern Michigan, where I'd spent so many childhood summers, wandering through eerily barren woods.

Sun streamed in, and the giant zinnias in our side yard seemed to stretch all the way to the sink. The unseasonably warm air brought mourning dove coos through the open window, and our clothes dotted with sweat.

My mother, in her sixties, looked younger than most of my friends' parents, though she was no longer thin. Her still naturally blonde hair shone in a short bob. She wore neat polyester slacks, a pastel scoop neck, and white sneakers. My blue jeans stained orange at the knees from the Virginia clay of my garden.

"Did Noah send out his application?" my mother asked, her voice conspiratorial. He was now a senior in high school, and my mother was accustomed to his unpredictability. Since he'd started middle school and free-fallen into premature puberty he'd started saying things like, "A family is a democracy, so why should you be able to tell me what to do?" and "Who voted you dictator?" Her tone said that she was wise to the exasperating tactics of this species called teenagers. She had used that same tone when she'd confided to me earlier, "Our punishment for being a teenager is having to parent one." It was an almost-whisper, the same soft voice I use myself, which makes people tell me to speak up. I leaned in to hear better.

"Yes," I said, "*finally*." Noah was applying to college as "early decision," which meant the deadline was the end of October. The previous day. "A minute before midnight."

"Did he let you look at it first?"

"I forced him to show me his essays."

"How'd you manage that?" If I'd leaned in further I might have heard an uncharacteristic edge in her voice. If I'd looked closely I might have noticed a smile that said, *Just wait until he moves away. Once kids grow up they never consult their mothers. About anything.*

I shrugged.

"What'd he write about?" My mother scrubbed the lentils I'd burnt on the bottom of the pan, mustering all her muscle to clean up my mess.

"Bugs," I said. "Bugs and trash. Can you believe it?"

"Is that bad?"

"You want to see?" I brought a paper copy down from my office and read aloud, "I would hear a sound and imagine bubble-wrap eyes and hundreds of wiener-dog legs that could crawl up my spine. I wouldn't look long enough to see if it was a centipede or a moth or a roach. I would simply flee."

"Fine, he wants to prove he doesn't need me," I said. "But I'm not just his mom, I'm a *writer*."

Only in hindsight is it clear how ridiculous this conversation was. I complained to my mother about my child because he had just done to me what I had already done to her. Without first consulting the person who could offer the most help, I sent out an essay of my own. My Father's Day piece.

I didn't have to dig deep to see why I didn't show that essay to my mother. I didn't want to remind her that she had witnessed cruelties: my father telling Louis he wasn't man enough and making him feel he didn't deserve to be his father's son.

I didn't see my comeuppance. I didn't ask my mother for her thoughts or advice, yet I magically expected my son would ask me.

We drank our coffee. I sighed. Paced. Steamed. Commiserated, mother to mother.

Then, abruptly, my mother plunked her cup on the kitchen island and cleared her throat. "Speaking of essays . . ."

I stopped puttering with the cabinets and pots, pulled up the stool, and braced for the moment I'd dreaded for months.

It took a while to coax out what she wanted to say. "I read the essay about your dad," she finally continued. "Aunt Mary saw the link on Facebook and sent it to me."

If my family had been home, I could have slipped into another room, claiming Ella needed me to find her a pair of socks or a hair-brush. The quiet in the kitchen made the bird coos sound like wails. All I could do was whisper, "Oh. I'm sorry."

Was I sorry I'd written the essay or that we'd all had to live through what it described? We sat stool to stool, staring into our cups.

"Was it . . . ?" This time she had to finish *my* sentence.

"True?"

I nodded.

She nodded back.

At least she didn't think I lied.

"It's true your dad took your sister hunting instead of Lou. It's true your dad was a man's man and Lou was . . . not. But is that enough . . ." She didn't have to finish the sentence. Was that enough to want someone *dead*?

"Lou has a photographic memory . . . ," my mother said.

Silently, I filled in the rest: *So he must be right.* My mother likes to mention my brother's amazing recall, a trait he inherited from our father, and I've always believed in this almost supernatural ability, but now I was beginning to wonder. I don't think Lou ever characterized himself that way. We forget what we need to forget, if we're lucky.

"You know," my mother said. "Emotions . . ."

She let her words trail off, but I knew what she meant. *Emotions are not the same as facts.*

Aloud I just said, "Yeah," then turned up my palms. Maybe all the answers would fall down through my kitchen ceiling like rain.

IT WAS ALL SAINTS' DAY. A perfect time to visit our local legend, Thomas Jefferson.

People talk about Jefferson in Charlottesville, anchored by the university he founded, as if he were alive. "Jefferson would want us to build the road around the park, not through it." "Jefferson would not let high-rises obscure the view of the Blue Ridge Mountains." Instead of "What would Jesus do?" people ask, "What would Jefferson do?" The father of our city. The father of our country. We have a way of turning long-gone fathers into mythic figures, don't we?

My mother and I piled into my Odyssey. Though I like to think I'm impervious to marketing, I bought the car for its name. Driving is a necessary evil if you don't live in New York City, but at least I could imagine each little errand an epic voyage.

Ten minutes later, we arrived at Monticello, the house Jefferson designed and inhabited. Buses filled the parking lot with tourists traveling from president's house to president's house, so many packed into a short stretch of Virginia. I pointed out a license plate from Texas, another from California, still trying, like an insecure adolescent, to impress my mother, to show her I live somewhere so desirable people travel hundreds of miles to visit.

A tour group walked behind us speaking Japanese. My mother, as usual, made an inventory of foreign cars versus American. She brightened into a smile whenever she saw a Ford or GM—always and everywhere, a Detroiter.

We boarded a shuttle up the mountain to the main house, neo-classical columns flanking the doorways. Inside, the tour guide, a birdlike woman my mother's age with a soft Virginia twang that made her seem both authentic and fake, like an actress chosen for the part because she was so good at playing herself, showed off Jefferson's inventions—a pantograph or "copying machine" (pens attached so two identical versions of a document are written at the same time), dumbwaiters for lifting wine from the cellar to the dining room, and self-opening French doors.

Our guide instructed us to admire Jefferson's multi-lingual library. "How many languages do you think he knows?" she asked, disconcertingly referring to him in the present tense.

I was tempted to say a hundred. I'd taken this tour before and knew the answer was six, but a hundred sounded just as implausible. I let an elderly woman with a walker guess instead. "Seven?"

"He learns Spanish on the boat when he returns to America from France, where he is ambassador," the guide explained. "Teaches himself Spanish by reading Cervantes in the original."

What a brilliant man, we were supposed to think, and I did. Years ago, I've heard, the tour would stop there, keeping Jefferson's moral contradictions out of public view.

But our guide continued, recounting the story of Sally Hemings, a slave Jefferson owned and bedded, the mother of some of his children, though his paternity was only recently acknowledged and she remained a slave.

"He writes against slavery," the guide said. "He plans on freeing his slaves, but he never does. Here is a man who championed the notion, 'All men are created equal.' But he forces slaves to build his own house. The house you're standing in right now."

After the tour we visited the family cemetery where the Hemings have not been reinterred, even though they have been acknowledged as descendants of our third president. My mother stared through the iron grates. I could almost hear her thoughts, maybe read the minds of all the sons and daughters, mothers and fathers gathered around us: *Every family has secrets.*

We trudged down the hill to the cafeteria at the visitors' center. Over soup and salad and tea, my mother said, "I guess it's best not to pretend anymore."

I almost spilled my Earl Grey.

"Best not to sugarcoat the past," she said.

"Yeah." Maybe my mother really did understand why I wrote my essay.

"But can you call someone a bad man, when he was just a man of his time?"

It took me a minute to realize she was talking about Jefferson. She might not have realized it, but I knew she was thinking about my father. We'd spent the morning talking about him in my kitchen, wondering if it were possible to be a great man, brilliant and charismatic, and deeply flawed at the same time.

"There's no excuse for owning slaves. It's immoral," I said. "I don't care if everybody else was doing it."

My mother sipped her soup. She hid her eyes in her spoon. We were surrounded by crowds, but they were strangers, so we were alone enough that she might feel free to talk. She confided in me only if no one else was listening.

I quieted. Stilled. Waited. Finally, I asked, "What do you think?"

"What he did was wrong, of course," she said. "But should we talk about it? Why bring it up, when for so many years nobody did? Why *now*?"

"Why not?" I stared into my food too.

"People might get hurt. The ones who thought . . . you know . . . he was a hero."

"People might get hurt by not telling the truth." I meant "What about the Hemings family? If we pretend that Jefferson was a hero, we deny those people the right to the truths of their own lives. We twist what happened to them into lies."

I also wanted to say, but couldn't yet form the words, "What are the consequences of hiding family truth? If we're too afraid to say the wrong things, we may avoid each other. Lose each other."

I couldn't help thinking of my sister.

I speared my salad, wiped the oily film from my mouth and hands, and my mother and I descended to the parking lot. On the way we passed a life-size bronze statue of Jefferson. "He's not as big as I expected," my mother said.

"No. They never are."

As we drove home in my minivan, I checked and rechecked the seatbelt across my shoulders, flicked my daytime lights on, confirmed the airbags were activated. Talking about my father had not killed me. Yet.

Where did my instinctive prohibition against talking about him come from? Did I think my mother would "kill" me by refusing to speak to me again? Am I paranoid because I keep thinking if I say the wrong thing people will decide never to talk to me again?

People like my sister. I sat on my front porch, sipping tea with my mother, and tried to remember.

The last time I saw Lynn, Noah was only five, Lynn's children a couple years younger, and my divorce not yet final. I'd flown to Denver from New York City to attend a conference for the special education publisher for whom I worked, tacking on a trip to my sister's house outside Colorado Springs. My mother joined us from Detroit, and I left Noah with her when I had to work.

As little girls my sister and I had been tender. Almost-twins, a year and a half apart, Lynn and I had shared strawberry pajamas and watermelon lip-gloss, whispering our secret fears that our mother might remarry and our clandestine crushes, deep into the night, our beds a few feet apart.

Then in junior high, we chose different tracks. She moved her bed to the basement and used *party* as a verb. I was enough of a nerd to point out that the word was a noun.

We'd both left Detroit, part of a mass exodus from a city leaking jobs. Our choices were two extremes: Manhattan then Brooklyn for me, rural Colorado for her. We both became wives and mothers, the first time, too young.

Lynn lived on the side of a craggy range, where bison and mountain lions roamed like squirrels and snow lingered into May. I'd visited several times, but this landscape still struck me as wild and exotic. She grilled us meat as big and pink as the cowboy sky at dusk.

Packed into my sister's Ford Explorer, we drove ten thousand feet to the summer snow on Pike's Peak. In my sundress, strappy sandals, and black leather jacket, I was equipped for little more than a stroll through Central Park. My suitcase, filled with pumps and suits, had no room for hiking boots.

We trekked through the Garden of the Gods, a landscape of giant red boulders, austere and unrelenting in its allure. Lynn was starkly beautiful too. She was nearing thirty but could have passed for seventeen, her mane of strawberry blonde hair flowing behind as she mounted mythically large rocks. Her denim short-shorts flaunted the muscles in the back of her thighs as she left me behind. In my inappropriate shoes.

At the Ghost Town Wild West Museum, the children pretended to pan for gold, and I thought they'd found it in their cousin-hood, the currency to keep our family together. Then, outside the fake saloon, I heard a shot. Then another.

The shoot-out, with actors costumed in full frontier regalia, was kitschy and stylized, John Wayne meets Disneyland. I couldn't resist the impulse to bring home a toy gun as a souvenir from this George Saunders-esque landscape, its pretend violence hovering somewhere near innocent, real, and surreal. When my sister saw the toy arsenal I'd purchased, she said, "You *trying* to raise a serial killer?"

Throughout the visit, I was too stressed to eat, worried about making another misstep and queasy from my divorce lawyer's barrage of messages. I must have picked at the meat Lynn heaped on my plate.

We pushed our children on the swings and pushed each other's buttons. "Crime is down in New York," I said. "The streets are safe."

But Lynn didn't believe me. "How can you send your kid to a public school," she asked, "full of gangs and guns and drugs?" She'd brought her own children to the wilderness to protect them from the urban dangers she'd been exposed to. She would homeschool them.

"You *want* them to be hermits?" I asked.

When I searched for silverware to set the table, Lynn snapped, "You couldn't ask me where it is? You have to find out for yourself?" When I offered to pay for gas, she said, "Do you always have to be in control?" She had driven us all the way to The North Pole, an amusement park where Santa granted our children's wishes as we banged into each other with bumper cars.

Lynn barked at her husband and our mother if they woke her up or not, since she always slept through the alarm. At a playdate, she reprimanded her best friend's lax discipline. I hoped these were just symptoms of sleep deprivation, from working the night shift till three in the morning. Her schedule would have jangled my nerves too. I couldn't have done what she did for a week, let alone year after year.

When Lynn drove us all to the airport, I was already planning the next visit in my head. We'd squabbled, as sisters sometimes do, but I'd considered the trip a success. The cousins had started to blend together, like the drawings they sketched and colored on all five of Lynn's wooden decks, overlooking nothing man-made for miles. All three of the children had whooshed down the backyard slide like one long child. The thin, alpine air made them extra dizzy and giggly. Then they danced to Dolly Parton, the soundtrack of my childhood.

As we prepared to take our leaves, my mother hugged Lynn goodbye, and I tried to do the same. Lynn backed away and crossed her arms on her chest.

"You won't hug me?" I said, at first light and teasing. Surely, she was playing. Her hands cupped her elbows, her arms locked shut. "Please," I finally begged.

I held back my tears until I was vacuum packed in my seat above the roar of the engine and had started distracting my son with a Transformer I'd purchased for the plane.

I was usually so adept at maintaining composure in front of him during the divorce, waiting till he fell asleep or I closed my office door at work to fall apart. When he asked why I was crying, I said, "Because I miss my sister." I didn't tell him that maybe much more than the visit was over.

At home, I put Noah to bed, then called Lynn and asked why she wouldn't give me a hug. We both cried, but I never really learned the answer. I hadn't made myself at home, she said. I hadn't seemed to like her food, which made her think I was too good for it. I'd bought a Pike's Peak sweatshirt but she bet I'd never wear it. Me and my fancy city clothes. Why had I refused her hospitality? she asked. She cited the way I offered to pay at restaurants and gas stations as an example of my refusal to let her do anything for me, to put myself in her debt, to trust her.

These small misunderstandings seemed so petty, cover-up for her real reasons. Reasons buried much too deep for me to reach through the phone.

The story I told myself was this: I'd learn more on my next trip, when we could hold each other skin to skin, like children.

I'm still waiting.

"MORE TEA?" I ASKED MY mother, then poured Earl Grey into a cup from the set she'd given me for my birthday. "You know," I said. "Lynn hasn't responded to my e-mails or cards in years."

My mother looked away.

I swallowed hard. "Why is she mad at me?"

"She doesn't wish you any ill," my mother said. "She took your dad's death real hard. She's cut herself off from her past because it hurts too much to think about it."

"So what should I do?"

She let out a gust of breath. She squirmed in her seat and shook her foot, crossed over her knee. "Just stop writing to her. There's no point."

"She told you that?" I clenched the armrests on my chair.

"No, but every time I mention your name, she pretends she doesn't hear."

"What about Lou?"

"If I say his name, she just walks away."

"I hate to think the next time I see her will be at a funeral," I said.

I expected my mother to reassure me, to brush away such an outlandish idea. But instead she said, "I'm sure when that happens, you'll be gracious, as always."

UNTIL MY MOTHER TOLD ME to give up on Lynn, I'd fooled myself into thinking I was number ten on her to-do list and she was still working on number nine. It was almost Christmas, and for the first time I didn't even send Lynn a card. My usual exchange of twelve tiny photos collaged on the cover with a few paragraphs of annual highlights is superficial and sentimental, I know. But these cards had given me the illusion that I was still connecting.

I considered jumping on a plane and landing on her doorstep. "Don't stalk her," Noah said. "Leave her alone."

Lynn was the last person who saw our father and the only live witness to his accident. Without talking to her again, I couldn't understand what had happened the night he died.

Yet I felt compelled to try.

I wrote another essay and sent it off, again without showing it to my mother. At the time I didn't realize why I was hiding my work from her. Now I see that I wanted to keep my own memories intact without adding her ideas to change them. Without having her chip away and revise the stories I told myself. The stories that kept me company for so many years.

I described the night my father died, when he took my sister hunting with him but might have taken me, had I been a boy. I wrote about our dog, Excalibur, who'd ridden in the Jeep with my father and sister and escaped unscathed. My father named our dog (*his* dog) after King Arthur's sword. Ex was fond of smelling flowers and offering sloppy kisses. He didn't live up to his name.

I wrote everything I could recall. But my only source was the fragmented memory of a seven-year-old.

My editor at *Narrative* magazine asked obvious questions I'd avoided confronting myself. How much was my sister hurt? What were her injuries? How exactly did the accident happen?

I couldn't call my mother and ask. Did I think she would yell? Never. But she might cry.

I sent her an e-mail instead, and she wrote back, a page and a half. More words than she had written me before, maybe more than she had written anyone.

My father's mother, Alma, was the family letter writer. She sent me frequent updates when I was in college, often tucked into a box of homemade cookies.

Early in my life, I equated my mother's lack of words with a lack of feeling. It has taken me years to understand how unfair that assessment is.

I cradled my arms on my desk, my head on my hands, and read.

Lynn was not hurt physically in the accident, my mother's letter said. She was in the back of the Jeep asleep. She was picked up from the side of the freeway by a couple who heard her calling "daddy." It was so foggy the couple didn't see her right away but heard her voice.

Then they saw our dad. He had been thrown from the Jeep and was lying on the highway. Lynn was sitting at the edge of the road calling out. She apparently woke up and must have walked outside the Jeep.

When asked why she stayed there at the side of the road, she said she had only one shoe on. Somehow her other shoe came off. If it weren't for the missing shoe she probably would have walked onto the highway and gotten hit by a car and killed.

Later she drew a picture of herself sitting beside the Jeep with only one shoe, tears coming down her face. My mother still has that drawing.

I exhaled short, choppy breaths from my chest, and out came every time my sister accused me of an unnamed crime. Out came her silence, her pretended deafness, her steely stare. I let all that go. It was all gone.

Then I breathed in the loose laces, the sneaker perhaps a too-big hand-me-down that slipped off in sleep, the shoeless foot that kept her safe. My poor little sister.

When I was seven and she was six, I was far too immature to understand what happened to her. I couldn't even cry for my father, let alone for Lynn. But decades later, all those pent-up tears came flooding.

My mother's e-mail also said Lynn told her she had survivor's guilt. All her life Lynn wished she had died with our father.

She tried. When she was fourteen, she overdosed on pills. "Of course you remember that," my mother told me. "It was on your sixteenth birthday. We were on our way to Grandma and Grandpa's house for your party, but we had to take Lynn to the emergency room instead."

I *didn't* remember. How was that possible?

My mother continued, "She told me, in the hospital, after they pumped her stomach, that she'd been trying to join your dad."

I don't know how long I sat with my head on my desk, paralyzed and alone. Finally, I rose and stumbled to the kitchen. "What is it?" my husband asked.

"A missing shoe." Thank God she lost her shoe. I might not have even been able to say that much.

A MISSING SHOE. A MISSING sister. What was the connection? I'd named my blog Walking on the Highway, without knowing why. Now I did.

Later, when I saw my mother in person, I asked, "Is that why Lynn doesn't want to talk to Louis and me—because she lived and Dad died?" That might explain a lot.

"I don't know," my mother said. "She doesn't talk about her feelings much," my mother said.

"Not even to you?"

"No."

She drank her tea, clinking her spoon against her mug, but I persisted.

"But what do you *think*?"

"You and Lou stuck together so much, she felt left out. And she always wanted to come along when you went to Jenny's house. Sometimes she said she felt like an only child."

THE STORY I ALWAYS TOLD myself was this: Lynn watched MTV and blasted heavy metal, which made her fit right in at school. Lou and I, prodigy and poet, were the weirdoes, pushed to the fringe. So we bonded together to convince ourselves we weren't aliens from outer space, like Robin Williams on *Mork and Mindy*, our favorite show. Lynn was the one who mocked the way we dressed and talked. She chose a vocational track to avoid the classes of teachers who already knew Lou and me, rejecting our intellectual interests as tame and effeminate. But maybe that's not the right story. It's certainly not the only one. Hers might be that we rejected her. I wish I had let her in, back then. I wish I could now. I want to remember myself as empathic and generous. But maybe I was just trying to survive.

Survivor's guilt. Post-traumatic stress disorder. Those words may be as close as I can come to explaining my sister.

Lynn tried to kill herself when I turned sixteen. I must have suppressed her suicide attempt. Just blocked it out.

Could I trust any of my memories, then? Maybe they were just stories I told myself. The one about the night my father died went like this.

IT'S TOO DARK TO WAKE, when my mother turns on my light and yells, "Get out of bed!" so I pull my Holly Hobby polyester coverlet back over my head and let out a moan. I don't expect her to bark commands.

The doorbell rings, and my mother turns on the lights but keeps the curtains closed. On normal Sundays, she lets me sleep in, since church begins at ten.

I pad out to the kitchen in my favorite pajamas, the ones I swear smell like jam, and follow my mother as she shuffles to answer the bell. "Why are people coming this early?" I ask.

"There's been an accident." She doesn't give me time to ask what happened to my father and my sister. She stands in front of the door and smooths her face, breathing into her hand to calm down, preparing to let the world in. I wait for more, but she just says, "Go on, get dressed," and shoos me away.

"What should I wear?"

"What you wore yesterday."

"It's dirty."

"Just go!" Normally she spoke so softly it wasn't clear she really wanted to be heard. Now her voice comes clipped, clear, and curt—the sound of adrenaline. Her long blonde hair, usually piled on top of her head with a hundred bobby pins, now hangs loose and tangled. She wears clothes from the night before too—pedal pushers and a red-and-white checked top, knotted at the navel. I'm proud of my pretty young mother.

She opens the door on the front landing, and my paternal grandparents, Alma and Kenneth, along with my Uncle Barry and Aunt Cora, pull her into a hug and let her lean on them. I scamper away, hover in the hall, hiding along the wall, willing myself to vanish like a ghost. Perhaps my mother fills the percolator with water and grounds, the simple, concrete task allowing her to focus her mind on a detail she can control when so much else is chaos.

I light into the bedroom my little sister and I share. Lynn's not there. I don't remember why she was chosen for the hunting trip. It's a question I've mulled over for years. Perhaps her eagerness. The answer could be as simple as that.

I slip on my red vinyl jumper, squeaky and speckled with dried Play-Doh that sticks in its cracks and creases. I try to scrape it with my fingernails. Years later, all I have to do is think of that dress and I can feel that night rubbing against my skin like a rash.

I sit at the kitchen table, waiting for my mother to pour me a bowl of Lucky Charms. The doughy smell of my dirty dress merges with the aroma of coffee and dried marshmallows. Everyone clutches a cup, and I don't understand why they don't just go back to sleep. The sun sticks below the surface.

In my memory, our house is full. With aunts, uncles, and cousins. Friends and neighbors. But recently my mother told me only my paternal grandparents and aunt and uncle came. Maybe I confused the night he died with the day of the funeral. At both, I felt crowded, hemmed in, jostled, barely able to move.

I follow my grandmother and mother into my nine-year-old brother's small bedroom. My grandmother stands straight against the wall, filling the room. In the corner, my mother crumples, knees to chin. I sit on the foot of the bed, my brother at its head.

His pillowcase of Halloween candy and the hollow chocolate bunny from Easter slumps undisturbed on his dresser. Louis' self-restraint is magical to me, weird to all the other kids. His control is strange enough to be a superpower. I always gobble my candy as quickly as I can.

A town of egg-shaped figurines clutter his floor. "Weebles wobble but they don't fall down," the jingle rings in my head. Louis doesn't play with army men, though. No G.I. Joe. Those toys languish in the closet.

"We're going to my house to make chocolate chip cookies." My grandmother's voice strains to keep its normal cheerful lilt. "Won't that be nice?" She wrestles clothes from the jammed dresser drawer, so close her flowered house dress rubs against my knees.

"My jumper's dirty," I say, still picking at it.

"Doesn't matter." My old world no longer exists, I know from her answer. My grandmother is meticulous about cleanliness.

"Get dressed quick." My grandmother hands my brother a striped shirt and jeans.

"Is Mommy coming with us?" Louis asks.

"No. She's going to the hospital to get your sister."

"An accident," I explain to my brother. For once, I know more than he does.

"Is she getting Daddy too?" he asks.

My grandmother pivots toward my mother. "I think it's time you tell them."

My mother snuffles, bites her lip, and covers her eyes.

"Get ahold of yourself. For their sakes."

This part I just learned, from my mother. She slips into the bathroom and emerges minutes later, those moments stretching like elastic, separating our old lives from our new ones. The time over the sink when she sobs, wipes her face, then dabs her cheeks with make-up is all my brother and I have left of our "before" time. Before she tells us.

After she re-enters my brother's bedroom, my mother squeezes on the bottom of the bed with me. My brother sprawls near the top. My grandmother stands close by, but I imagine everyone else staying in the kitchen.

"Daddy was hurt too bad to live," my mother says, sucking in her breath, looking away to avoid crying in front of us. She later told me this conversation was the most difficult of her life. "A deer ran in front of his Jeep on the road." A deer killed my dad. Impossible. I'd seen *Bambi.* Men killed deer with their guns. Deer are vegetarian. My father taught me the fancy word for that: herbivore. A lion could have got him. A tiger maybe. That I might believe.

I don't cry. I don't know why. *I can kiss my own boo-boos.*

My father used to say, "Don't cry or I'll give you something to cry about."

THE DÉCOR I IMAGINE FOR the funeral home is dark wood and stiff benches with thin red velvet cushions, a contrast to the soft fabrics and muted colors in our house. But maybe the hard furniture is just a reflection of my discomfort, my not wanting to be there.

I know this room is meant to look like a rich person's parlor I've seen on TV. It also reminds me of church, though more glossy than my down-to-earth Free Methodist one. I would have used the word *pretentious* if I'd known what it meant.

The crowd is big enough to fill the room with hot air. Members of our church squeeze in, our neighbors and teachers. When someone dies so young, it's a tragedy, or at least a spectacle, for the whole community.

My grandmother summons my brother, sister, mother, and me and tells us to touch my father's skin. I don't want to. My grandmother grew up during the Depression on a farm where her father was the local butcher and the local veterinarian. She had no patience for squeamishness.

Streams of people lean on the walls of the viewing room, standing in line for their turn to see my father or talk to us, his survivors. His casket stands near the middle of the far wall and that's where we lurk, while everyone else shuffles in and out.

My grandmother, the matriarch, chose my mother's dress. In my memory, it is always black, high necked, and pleated down to the knee, not like the short, straight numbers girls wore in the seventies. My mother's long, blonde hair glistens in a French twist, but today she hasn't put on the bright lipstick she applied without fail all other days right before my father came home.

She'd come of age in the era of women's lib but spent those bra-burning years changing diapers instead. She never protested, in any sense of the word—didn't march on Washington or complain about her situation. Years later I learned that my paternal grandfather had urged her to give him power of attorney after my father's death, not believing her capable of writing her own checks and handling even routine paperwork. "I was in my twenties," she told me, "but he treated me like you kids." Then she added, because I know how much she loved and appreciated him, "He meant well, though."

My grandmother presses me so close to the coffin that the slippery gloss of the lacquered wood slides against my scratchy dress. The smell of lilies mixes with Mr. Clean, making the flowers seem artificial even though they're real. The velvet lining, the shiny veneer, the bouquets, and his fancy clothes, a black suit I can't remember ever seeing him wear, makes me wonder if the man inside is really my father.

He should have chosen a more rustic resting place. He was a man's man, who enjoyed answering the door in his boxer shorts to shock our prim and proper next-door neighbor, Mrs. Vann. He could have worn blue jeans and a work cap, sweaty and greasy from crawling under the bellies of cars.

In the coffin, his sleeves are crossed on his chest, his missing right hand covered with more flowers. He is in costume. So am I, my fine hair slicked back, my too-tight patent leather Mary Janes pinching my toes. Are all these people waiting for me to cry on cue?

My gregarious, redheaded paternal grandmother, who was exposed to all forms of bodily unpleasantness as a nurse's aide, pats my father's face then says to me, "You do it."

When I bristle and pull away, she grabs my hand and plunks it on his cheek. Even though the coroner performed his magic with make-up and chemicals to make my father look alive, one touch confirms he isn't.

He feels like cold chicken skin.

My mother, right beside me, seems small and silent enough to disappear with my father. Her clavicle pokes out like a wishbone. If I could pull the winning half of that bone, I would wish for a cuddle in bed and the extra pillow she always fluffs under my head when I'm sick.

I withdraw my hands from the coffin as if from a lion's mouth, then my grandmother makes my siblings, mother, and me stand together. Mourners greet us with hugs, lowered heads, and sometimes tears. I want to crouch in a corner and immerse myself in *Charlotte's Web,* retreating into a story I can understand.

Eyes are on me, I'm convinced, rubberneckers at an accident. Bone-deep self-consciousness is the only emotion I am able to feel at that moment. The urge to disappear, to hide from stares, absorbs me totally.

Crying would be a relief, but I can't. All my circuits are down. I stare at my shiny shoes, at the red cushions, at a spider web in a far-off corner glistening with menace. Anything to avoid thinking about why I am there. My grandmother's insistence that I touch my father seems ghoulish, macabre, even cruel.

Now, though, I'm grateful. If I didn't have that visceral memory of his permanently frigid skin against the burning pulse of my thumb, his death might have become an abstraction for me. I might not have believed he was gone.

In the weeks and months that follow, my teacher, Sunday School leader, pastor, Brownies den mother, neighbors, and well-meaning relatives keep asking me if I cried. Even kids at school. I'd always been proud of being a good student, compliant and cooperative, but I keep failing to give the right answer.

I cry easily now, making up for lost time. Dinner has to come before the movie or I'll be cutting my steak with a face covered with mascara and mucus. I cry at weddings, of course, funerals and baby showers, though I draw the line at birthday parties. I can't finish a book in a cafe or I'll end up blubbering in front of the barista. If someone dies in the story, you'll hear my sobs all the way on the other side of the Atlantic.

But back then, my eyes remain dry. I worry that I'm becoming a callous kid. Thick skinned. I wish someone told me that mourning is a skill, something I could learn over time.

My FIRST DAY BACK TO church after the funeral, my Sunday School teacher asks, "How do you feel?"

"I feel bad," I say, meaning "I feel like I *am* bad." Bad and stubborn. Unwilling to believe, as the grown-ups said, that my father was gone for good.

When I finally return to school, months later, Mrs. Taylor, my second-grade teacher, turns me into an exotic specimen under a microscope. For show and tell we sit crisscross applesauce in a circle on the braided rug next to her desk. She allows everyone else to talk about their Christmas vacations. Laura got a pogo stick. Michael got a BB gun. Kim's cat had kittens, black and white with little mitten paws. Kim holds up a picture. "We went door to door to give them away," she says.

"Aw," we coo collectively.

"Roy, it's your turn," Mrs. Taylor says. "You got a new baby sister for Christmas, right?" We all know his mother lives down the street from her.

"But that's not what I asked for!" Roy says, and Mrs. Taylor laughs that sweet tea laugh of hers, ladylike sounds careful never to burst out of their corsets. We kids don't laugh. We don't want a baby sister either.

Round and round the circle we go. Maybe if I sit completely still she'll skip me. I stare at the frilly cursive alphabet above the chalkboard, each letter with a picture, A for apple, Z for zebra.

Inspirational posters, one with a kitten dangling from a tree advising us to "Hang in There." A bulletin board with scenes of sleds and snowmen proclaiming "Winter Wonderland." Another board with our mitten-shaped state surrounded by water, with a cut-out of the Frosted Flakes mascot. "Tony the Tiger says The Great Lakes are Gr-r-r-reat!" On the far wall near our coat rack hangs a poster of John Wayne saying "Courage is being scared to death, but saddling up anyway.

"Children, you know Sharon's been absent several months. You know why, right? Her father went up to heaven to be with the angels. Can you tell us about that, sweetheart?"

I stare at John Wayne, dumb.

Mrs. Taylor waits. Saunters over to me, hands on hips, bracelets jangling, her heavy lilac perfume making me stifle a sneeze. "It's your turn now. Tell us." Her voice shines a spotlight on me.

"I got a toy piano for Christmas," I say.

"Oh, honey. That's not what I meant. Tell us about your daddy."

I don't want to. But I can't tell her that. I can't say anything.

"Do you feel sad?" Mrs. Taylor asks, her jeweled reading glasses dangling around her neck, her voice tinged with age and a lingering Southern accent, like so many people I know, midwestern transplants from Appalachia.

"Yes," I finally say, because I can tell that's the right answer. I don't really know how I feel, but now I would call it numb. I don't cry, and I know this disappoints people, so I try. I owe them that. Envelopes with cards and money arrive in the mail, their charity making me feel poor.

In the story I tell myself about returning to school for the first time, my father's premature death turns me into a tragic children's book character. Think Snow White, Cinderella, Hansel & Gretel, James and the Giant Peach. My daughter Ella tells me it's a cliché to begin a children's book with a parent dead on the first page, it happens so much. The authors seem to be telling their readers, "Count yourself lucky. At least you're not an orphan."

Likely my second-grade teacher, by spotlighting me, was trying to get me to open up, to acknowledge my feelings, as part of the grieving process. I am sure she meant well. But what it felt like to me then was that she was trying to say to the rest of the class, "Stop complaining you didn't get what you wanted for Christmas. At least you're not *her*."

THE STORY I DIDN'T TELL my class, about what I got for Christmas, goes like this.

My family doesn't have enough money or space for such an extravagant gift, but I'm delusional. I want a grand piano. I don't specify, secretly expecting an upright. On Christmas morning I unwrap a tiny instrument. Light enough to lift with one hand.

I didn't ask for a *toy*.

I leave my mother and the afterschool snacks she placed on the table, then climb up on my flimsy piano bench, still near the Christmas tree. "It's not *real*," I say to no one. Then I stomp and break the leg. My throat itches, my breath comes quick and shallow and loud. Finally, I'm able to cry.

THIS TIME, IN MY DREAM, I'm Emily in *Our Town*, a play I performed in at fourteen. Of course, I forget my lines. I don't remember her saying, from the afterlife, "Good-by, world. Good-by, Grover's Corners . . . Mama and Papa. Good-by to clocks ticking . . . and Mama's sunflowers. And food and coffee. And new-ironed dresses and hot baths . . . and sleeping and waking up. Oh, earth, you're too wonderful for anybody to realize you."

I'M TRYING TO REMEMBER LOOKING into my father's face. The visual I substitute is his grave. That man-sized rectangle of grass became my father's portrait in my head, my memories of him morphing into memories of Memorial Days.

On every holiday, my family visited Michigan Memorial Park in Flat Rock. My paternal grandparents went every Sunday, and often we trailed along. On the drive, I watched the asphalt turn to dirt, the space between the houses magnify. We called Flat Rock the country.

While our mother and grandmother slipped snapdragons and baby's breath into the headstone's vase (my grandmother grew flowers in her garden just for this purpose), my brother, sister, and I fed an apple to the horse on the other side of the fence, then crouched at the edge of the grave as close as we could without treading on it.

When I picture the cemetery, I see myself standing on the hill near the swan-filled lake. I'm eight, nine, and ten, my Mary Janes sinking into the wet dirt. I live in the blur between the real and imagined, almost expecting my father to reach up and teach me to snowmobile through the woods at breakneck speed, to start my own machine parts company and become a millionaire, to light the road on fire, to stick it to "the man."

At eleven, twelve, and into my teens, I'm wearing white Keds or Salvation Army red cowboy boots in the cemetery snow, waiting for my father to rise from underground, as if he'd just been a bear in hibernation. Then to tell me it's finally time to teach me his tricks, that I'm old enough to learn to fix every broken object in our house or garage or life, with his welder's fire on a stick.

Our brains, for self-preservation and healing, create holes where traumatic memories hide. I want to find them.

I want to smell the coffee my mother brewed on the night of the accident and lick the bowl of chocolate chip cookie dough my grandmother made to distract us. I want to taste the sour paste in the back of my throat, to fill in the missing pieces of my own story, to figure out why I have so many holes.

Am I who I am *because* of these holes? If I had other missing pieces, would I have become a different kind of person? If my memories change, will I change too?

My father will always be the age he was at the funeral home. But I still had time to grow up.

Part 1

Part 2
The Y

Overleaf: (*top*) My parents' wedding reception, January 10, 1965; (*bottom*) My first trip with James, April 2001

April 2012

WHEN I TOLD MY FRIENDS I was spending spring break in Detroit, many muttered, "Never been," their tone implying that the city had come to represent, for them, the anti-tourist destination.

I'm tired of the easy cliché of Detroit as the emblem of a bygone prosperous era, of a rust-belt city bleeding manufacturing jobs, a casualty of competition overseas and the exponential growth of automation. I cringe when I see the place I grew up in treated as a spooky joke, as it was in a recent vampire art house film I saw with my son. In *Only Lovers Left Alive*, the city itself is one of the undead, its desolate streets and abandoned buildings the perfect backdrop for haunted creatures breaking into hospital blood banks. I'm weary of "ruins porn," the recent trend of artists photographing hollowed-out, graffitied train stations and theaters. Though I'll admit to being lured in myself, at times. It's hard not to gawk at a train wreck.

I want people to see the city with fresh eyes. By "people," of course, I mean myself.

A decade ago, when my mother married my stepfather Joe, she moved forty minutes across town to Eastpointe, on the eastern border of Detroit. This suburb was called East Detroit until a few years ago, when the word "Detroit" became so pejorative the citizens voted to change their identity. Like the streets of Lincoln Park, where I grew up (a suburb in the southwest, in an area called Downriver), the ones in Eastpointe are lined with one-story houses. I've lived in larger apartments, but as a child, my house didn't feel small.

After the recession in 2008, foreclosure signs mushroomed on my mother's block. "The worst," she told me, "is when people steal the copper pipes. Just across the street. It's like there's no law and order anymore." My stepfather Joe cooked the first night, grilled chicken and Rice-A-Roni. We thanked him for his kindness. He's never been anything but kind. He married my mother, though, when I was already a mother myself, so it's hard to think of him as anything but my mother's fourth husband. The second, in my teens, lasted two years, when nine people lived in our house. It's a period I try to forget. The third husband, in my twenties, lasted only months, and I can't even remember his name.

Joe, a natural raconteur, is as garrulous as my mother is quiet. He douses us with a genial buzz of sports statistics, recipes, and fishing lore. We all avoid economics, though my husband teaches it. We don't talk about current events. I've heard Joe thinks Barack Obama is the devil, so I keep my conversation skimming lightly on the surface. The last thing I want is to argue with someone who takes such good care of my mother.

After she retired from the deli counter at a gourmet market (she'd been downsized at the bank where she and Joe met), my mother started watching every Tigers game on TV. We surprised her with tickets to the second game of the season. Joe chose to stay home, but the rest of us drove to Comerica Park, the six-year-old ball field Downtown, about a mile north of the old historic Tiger Stadium. As we walked to the huge sports complex, my mother pointed out the YWCA where she lived for a year after high school.

Every time we passed the Y, she beamed. As a kid, I used to visit her at work in the summer, and we'd eat at the subsidized bank cafeteria or walk a block or two for a Coney Island hotdog, a fat frank loaded with chili, onions, and mustard—a Detroit specialty.

She'd point. "I used to live at the Y. Right there."

"I *know*," I'd say. I never asked why she kept walking me past the Y, what drew her to this nondescript brick building. What was so special about a bedroom with a shared toilet down the hall?

I'm sure it was better than her childhood home in Ecorse, a suburb just down the river from where I grew up. I'd been in my mother's childhood home only a few times, since Dorothy, the maternal grandmother we called Granny, disowned my mother after she married my father. Everything about the house felt claustrophobic and stifling.

After the Y, she moved into an apartment my father chose. The room at the Y was hers alone.

On game day, we passed that room and tried to squint through the window. Then we entered the stadium, a city within a city, offering microbrews and hummus, a Ferris wheel, carousel, and giant stone statues of tigers carrying baseballs in their mouths. Every seat was sold, 50,000 fans in caps embroidered with the team's curlicued logo, a gothic letter "D." We wore them too.

From our seats above home plate, we watched Prince Fielder hit his first two home runs with the Tigers after signing on, with much fanfare, in the offseason. Miguel Cabrera hit his own two. The water jetting from the home run fountain geysered up. It's not often success feels so inevitable, every expectation fulfilled. The final score: Red Sox 0, Tigers 10.

Nothing could spoil an afternoon like this. Except my teenage son.

Noah is a self-described nerd. His only sport is Ultimate Frisbee. He's not a jock or a sports fan. And yet, halfway through the game he removed the Tigers cap my mother bought him and started rooting for the Red Sox. Why do we sometimes give up on the place our people came from?

Maybe I needed to ask myself.

The sight of my own blood rooting for the enemy made me want to hide in the bathroom for the rest of the game. Noah reminded me too much of my teenage years, counting the days till I could leave Detroit.

The Tigers scored again, and the geyser squirted up to the clouds. Ella passed me peanuts, but I couldn't eat. Each home run made my stomach sour. Why?

I WAS IN HIGH SCHOOL when the Tigers were at their peak. They'd won thirty-five of their first forty games, something no team had done before. People said they were not just the best team that year, but the best *ever*.

Sports columnist George Cantor, in the *Detroit News,* wrote back in 1984, "It's 1968 all over again, the last time the Tigers won the World Series, when Detroiters could stop thinking about the race riots that turned downtown stores into empty shells a year earlier. This time it's all the factory lay-offs that people hope a baseball win will white-wash over."

The Tigers went all the way to the World Series that year. Then they won.

I saw the game on TV, and it was like the ball dropping on Times Square on New Year's Eve. Multiplied by a million. It felt like *I* had won. We Detroiters had beat those uppity, crunchy, sunny San Diego Padres ourselves.

But then it happened. It *was* 1968 all over again—the 1968 riots, redux. The crowd outside the stadium, about 100,000, mixed with the 50,000 ticket-holding fans to create chaos. Fans set police cars on fire and threw bottles. Teenagers, mostly white kids from the suburbs on a rare visit to the city, blocked buses on their routes and jumped on top of them. At least one person was killed. Many were injured. When I retrieved the old newspapers from the day after the final 1984 game, I saw that the damage was worse than I'd remembered.

THE CURRENT GAME AGAINST THE Red Sox ended, Noah's boos drowned by cheers. We glided down the aisles, on to Woodward, passing the once-grand Fox Theater.

The city became a sea of mostly white suburbanites. The neighborhood just north of the stadium, between the river and university, was newly dubbed Foxtown, an "urban village." A giant sports bar called Hockeytown dominated the landscape, and a dozen baseball-related eateries surrounded the stadium. Outside this bubble, though, lay empty lots and hollowed-out buildings. A few days earlier, *The Detroit News* had run an article on the city's feral fields, showing that abandoned, empty lots in Detroit were now so sprawling, the entire city of Paris could fit inside them. Although the piece ran on April 1, it was not an April Fool's joke.

We drove half a mile to Art Cafe on Cass Avenue, near the Wayne State campus. *Metro Times*, Detroit's alternative newspaper, called Art Cafe "the best place to take visitors from New York." We passed a hair salon called Curl Up and Dye, one of the only establishments on the street with a sign at all.

Art Cafe looked so much like an empty storefront from the outside that at first Noah hesitated to leave the car. "Don't you think it's a little too sketchy?" he asked. But inside, the restaurant, airy like a Brooklyn loft, was hung with hip, elegant drawings.

The menu offered lentil burgers, micro greens, and organic golden beets from one of the farms that have reclaimed empty lots from former residential neighborhoods. Outside the restaurant-oasis, the cityscape was deserted.

In other rust-belt areas, like Dayton, Ohio, manufacturing jobs were returning. But not in Detroit. I could barely stand to read the paper when I was in town, the news was so bad back then.

Chrysler's new Jefferson North plant had recently opened. But just blocks away we could see, as we drove from Art Cafe back to my mother's house, some of America's worst urban devastation, acre upon acre of vacant land and burned-out stores. The city that was home to nearly two million people in the 1950s was now down to 700,000. More than a third of them lived in poverty.

How would my father have reacted to what his city had become? The city his parents had migrated to from the country, with its promise of better jobs and more prosperous futures.

I know it's absurd. He was just one man. Yet I can't help imagining—*believing*—that if he'd lived, Detroit might have continued to thrive too. He had ambitious plans. He was a man of action. He never let obstacles, like a missing hand, get in his way. He was going to change the world. Or better yet, make sure it *didn't* change.

Maybe my father was still alive.

That was my first impression, my mind playing wishful thinking tricks on me, the next day when we visited Uncle Barry. Two brothers who were better friends, who loved each other more, you couldn't find in the world. That was the story I'd heard, though they'd always seemed an odd pair to me—Barry playful and affectionate, my father serious and stern.

My aunt and uncle had moved to rural Carleton, almost an hour away from the city. When I was growing up, they lived in the suburbs, as we did, and we saw them frequently, together with their three boys, my cousins.

As a child, I had always envied their lives, the fact that their family wasn't broken up the way mine was. I had romanticized them, thinking that their lives must be perfect. As an adult, I learned that they have all had to deal with the same kinds of problems everyone does.

Now I saw what I meant by perfect. Their father didn't die.

The youngest of my three cousins opened the door for us after we pulled into the driveway and rang the bell. My aunt led us to the living room, where she'd spread an array of cookies. She is in her sixties but looks much younger, as pretty now as in my memories from forty years ago.

My mother sat, then shot up again after Barry entered the room. "I'm not sitting in your chair, am I?"

"It's all yours." Barry squeezed into a corner of the couch, something I couldn't imagine my father would ever do.

Noah and Ella sampled every cookie in sight. "I could bring out cinnamon buns," Cora said.

"Otherwise we'd starve," Barry said with a boyish smile.

BARRY BEGAN SHARING STORIES ABOUT the world of welding and what it was like to pipeline in Alaska. He was trying to retire, but his skills were rare and people kept calling to beg him to take just one more job. Ella pulled out a notebook and began jotting down words and phrases, playing reporter. My uncle's stories fascinated her, and so did his gift for colorful phrases like "tight as tree bark." Her way of figuring out the world is to write it down.

"I bet you read a lot," Barry said to Ella. "Just like Jerry." My father.

He looked at me. "Always a book. You kids got that book learning from him."

Hearing my uncle invoke my father made me wonder how many of my memories came from Barry's stories. Unlike my mother, he loved to sprinkle my father into anecdotes. Jerry this. Jerry that.

Like my father, Barry always loved restoring old machines, for which he has a gift. He told us he still had the Ford Model B pickup that my father and his cousin Everett bought together when they were teenagers. Over the years, it has passed in ownership between Barry, my father, and Everett.

"I've been fixing up an old tractor," Barry said. "Got it out of storage from Up North." He rallied Noah and Ella to follow him. "Want to give it a spin?"

We all walked out to the pole barn and watched Barry pull the drop cloth off the old red tractor, oil it and check its moving parts, then start it up and move it out to the grass. "Climb on my lap," he said to Ella. Ella jumped up, and together they toured the property on the old tractor.

Barry showed off his Kitty Kat snowmobiles. His welding machine, his rig, the equipment he took to the pipelines when he hauled out to far-off places like Alaska on his jobs. He told more stories. Ella was so rapt she forgot to write them down.

Later, as we were driving home, my mother started to cry. She rarely broke down in front of me. Hers were quiet tears trying to hide themselves.

I leaned in. "You OK?"

"I miss him," she said.

At first I didn't know who she was talking about.

"That tractor. He loved that thing." Of course. She meant my father.

"Ella riding on it . . . He would have . . ." She paused. Caught her breath. Looked out the back window. The house had disappeared from sight. "He would have loved . . ."

I silently filled in my mother's blanks. He would have loved to have met his granddaughter. My father would have loved to see how much she is like him.

Noah looked out the window at the scenery of fields and farms. Ella read, aware of nothing beyond her book. Neither of my children saw me reach over to grab my mother's hand.

The next day, I woke at dawn and heard the bench swing squeak in the backyard. I left James in bed and slipped out to join my mother. She shot up. "Want some tea?"

"I'll get it myself."

"Here, take this seat," she insisted, moving to a hard metal chair.

"You take it."

"No, you."

I had to laugh at our competition over who could be more accommodating. Finally, we squeezed in together. The sun poked up a little pink. The house—the whole neighborhood—still slept.

"Sorry about Noah spoiling the game yesterday," I said.

"He's a teenager. What do you expect?"

The grass, wet with dew, smelled like wild green onions. Oil lingered in the air from the garage or leaky cars parked on the street. My mother and I shivered. "Let me get you another sweater," she said.

"No, I'm fine." I stuck my fingers down the back of my neck to warm them.

She said, "When Louis and Lynn were teenagers, I thought someone would get killed. You remember."

I didn't. I sipped my tea and tried, though.

"They fought like cats and dogs. One of them would have to go live with your grandparents, I kept thinking. Couldn't figure out which one, or I would have done it."

"I knew they fought," I said. "But not like that."

"Hormones," she said.

"Hormones?"

"They make people do crazy things. I had postpartum depression," she said. "Nobody called it that then. Thought I was going cuckoo."

"You never told me."

"People didn't talk about it. Thought I was going insane during menopause too."

I could have put my response on repeat. You never told me, you never told me, you never told me.

"It was right after I married Joe. I'm surprised he didn't want a divorce."

For most of my adult life, any news about my mother I'd discover only months later, and often from another source. I'd find out, too late, that she'd been dangerously ill, that she'd married somebody I'd never met, or divorced him almost as fast. Or that an aunt or uncle had died. But here, in the space of half an hour, I was learning more about her than I had in decades.

Something had changed since I broke the taboo against talking about my father. Since the conversation in my kitchen the day after Halloween. Since our trip to Monticello.

Since I went looking for my father. And found my mother instead.

I DREAMED I WAS IN the *Wizard of Oz* and, again, couldn't remember my lines. When I awoke I couldn't even recall which character I was supposed to play. Was my forgetfulness a lack of courage, brains, or heart?

A FEW MONTHS LATER, IN June, my mother flew in from Detroit for Noah's high school graduation. She was the only extended family member who did.

On commencement day, we cleaned up the lunch dishes together at my house, and I asked her about her own ceremony. She said, "Do you want to look at some pictures?"

I slid my album off the shelf and waited for the photos to prompt her. We sat at my dining room table in our hundred-year-old Craftsman-style house, in a room I love, with red walls and vintage wallpaper borders, dark wood molding, pocket doors, and built-in bookcases. We were already dressed in our proud family-of-the-graduate clothes—a black flowered dress for me, a pink tunic and black slacks for her. From the windows we could see an explosion of orange daylilies lining the side of our house. Ella and her friend Dorsey shot hoops in our driveway. The metal creak of the ironing board opening told me James was pressing a linen shirt to wear to the ceremony, less than an hour away. Noah was already at the auditorium, preparing.

My mother and I leafed through the photo album my paternal grandmother had given me at my own high school graduation. The book begins with my parents' prom, proceeds to their graduation, then their wedding, the events presented as inevitable chapters of a predictable life.

"My own mother didn't come to my graduation," my mother said. Of course, I should have known. Dorothy, or Granny, as we called her, suffered from a nonspecified but severe mental illness all her adult life. When we kids were old enough to answer the phone, even after our father was dead, Granny used to call and tell us to run away from home. That's how I knew she was ill. Paranoid. Delusional. Or, as I would have said then, "crazy."

We couldn't attend many family gatherings because Dorothy didn't want to see my mother who, I realize now, must have felt like a half-orphan too.

"Grandma and Grandpa came to my graduation," my mother said. My father's parents, Alma and Kenneth.

"You were living with them then?"

She nodded. "They were good to me."

Like second parents. Alma taught her to cook and bake pies and made the first birthday cake my mother had in her life, for her eighteenth birthday, angel food with frosting. She made her a quilt as soon as she started dating my father. I wasn't surprised. Alma made quilts and afghans and cakes for all of us. She nursed us on sick days home from school. Kenneth ferried us to doctors and dentists, taught us how to whittle, and shoveled our snow.

"So Dad had already given you an engagement ring?" I asked. "The diamond I'm wearing?" My mother had passed the diamond on to me, and I wore it as part of my own wedding/engagement ring set.

"Yes," she said. "But, you know, I gave it back."

Then how did she give it to me? I opened my mouth but couldn't say a word.

We turned the page and I noticed, again, that no photo exists of the actual wedding. We looked at the picture of the reception and avoided each other's eyes.

In the photo, my parents stand next to each other in the middle of the frame, knife poised above the cake, ready to cut. My father wears a dark suit. The color is faded, but I can imagine his wavy red hair, his bright green eyes. My mother looks lovely but serious in a short white dress with a pleated skirt, hands behind her back. The couple squeezes against the wall in my grandparents' basement, in front of a dining room table. The scene looks more like a Thanksgiving dinner than a fancy wedding reception. I never questioned the modest nature of the gathering. They wanted to save money, and I always admired that. I'm frugal too.

"Do you know why your dad looks angry in this picture?"

I shook my head. I'd never asked myself that question. His eyes gazed intently, his mouth pursed tightly in almost every picture I'd seen. I don't remember ever seeing him smile.

"He was upset," my mother explained, "because I'd just asked for a divorce."

I rubbed my eyes and dislodged a contact. I didn't rise to fix it though. Maybe everything would look better half-blurry.

I don't know if I said anything, but I didn't need to. It seemed as if my mother had been waiting my whole life for the right moment to tell me this story. Though, for me, the timing wasn't perfect. I couldn't imagine being able to rise from my chair for the rest of the day, let alone move through hours of celebrations.

My throat tightened. The soreness starting at the base of my clavicle spread all the way up to my ears. A rawness in my throat, like rust.

But my mother sat still, hands in her lap, eyes on her knees. She'd had decades to come to terms with the story of their wedding ending almost as soon as it began—not a few minutes, like me. The lines in her face relaxed.

"Why did you want a divorce?" I finally asked. We both stared at the photo.

Bounce. Bounce. The basketball pounded outside.

"I wasn't ready to be married," she said. "I was too young and immature. I guess I wanted to try life on my own for a while. And I looked at how my own parents treated each other and didn't want that."

"So why did you agree to get married in the first place?" This was the question I'd asked myself all my life. They seemed like such an unlikely couple. Before she could answer, though, she had to rewind. All the way back to their first date. I leaned back in my chair, trying to be quiet and listen. I crossed and uncrossed my legs. I cupped my chin in my hands. Then I willed myself to still. And waited. Finally, this is the story she told me.

On her seventeenth birthday my father gave her a wrapped box with a necklace in it and took her to see *West Side Story*. A tale of tragic lovers that ends with death. A cautionary tale? A prediction? I wish my parents had chosen *My Fair Lady* instead. Or, better yet, *The Sound of Music*. I want to whisper these suggestions in their ears. I want to beg them. Please.

They dated only a couple times before Dorothy, my mother's mother, forbid her to see my father again.

Dorothy called him a freak with one hand. She called him Hitler because of his mustache. She said he would not be able to support a family. (Later, he was driven to prove her wrong, which was why he worked such long hours.)

My mother was a high school junior working most weekends and after school from five to midnight. She asked my father to drive her home, and this form of clandestine dating continued until she turned eighteen. For her birthday he gave her another wrapped box. She had hoped for a second necklace, but it was a ring. An engagement ring. She wasn't ready for such a big step, but she didn't say so. She was used to doing what people expected her to.

She wore the ring on a chain under her clothes until Dorothy saw it. Days later she came home from school and Dorothy said her things were on the back porch and told her to move out.

She left the house and called my father from a pay phone at a nearby drug store. He drove her to the house where he lived with his parents, Alma and Kenneth. The next day, she rented a room from two brothers and their wives for ten dollars a week, drawing on the $500 she'd saved from working those two previous years at the root beer stand. She stayed there a couple of months until one night, the two brothers were drinking and got into a knife fight. Again, she walked to the nearest pay phone and called my father. That's when he moved her into his parents' house, where she stayed in the attic.

Alma drove my mother to school on her way to work as a nurse's aide at Outer Drive Hospital and picked her up after work. This routine continued till my mother's graduation.

In early June, my mother gave my father back his engagement ring. She said he did nothing wrong, she just needed to be free. He didn't come to her graduation because she'd already broken up with him. But his parents came. She lived in their house.

She wanted to move to an apartment, but Kenneth said that first she had to get a good enough job. That October she began working as a stenographer at Michigan Mutual Insurance Company on Adams Street downtown. She rented a room at the YWCA on Witherell. The Y we passed by so often. The Y she always looked at with so much longing. As always when she mentions the Y, her eyes lit up.

She started to glow. As she inhaled, then gazed off into the distance, I could see her imagining her dream house: A tiny box of a bedroom, with a minuscule communal kitchen and bathroom in the hall. "There's nothing like living by yourself. Making your own decisions," she said.

"Why'd you leave?" I'd never asked before. The answer had always seemed obvious—to marry my father. But nothing seemed obvious anymore.

I gripped the right side of the photo album, and she held the left. We were almost holding hands. If anybody walked into the room, she might cut our confidences short. I willed James not to walk downstairs, Ella not to rush in and ask for a glass of water.

My mother remained happily single until after someone she was dating broke up with her. Whenever something bad had happened before—when Dorothy had made her move out or the two brothers she rented from had a knife fight—she had called my father, and he made sure she was safe. He was always there for her.

"It sounds cuckoo," she said, "but I called him then too. To tell him about my break-up."

She hadn't meant to talk about marriage, but she was on the rebound and wasn't thinking straight. They filled out the marriage license form and took a blood test. My father rented a furnished apartment on Montcalm just off Woodward, downtown.

She continued living at the Y. Then one day, my father called her at work and said he would take her to lunch and to pick up the license. She had no idea that lunch would segue into a wedding. They bought two matching gold bands at Sears, then drove to the Free Methodist Church in Lincoln Park.

By that time, my mother really wanted to back out, but she was afraid it was too late. The pastor asked them a few questions, then took them from his office into the church and proceeded with the marriage ceremony. "How do I get out of this?" was the question that repeated in her head, without an answer. "That definitely was not a good way to start a marriage," she told me. "I did him a disservice by marrying him under those circumstances. He deserved much better. Perhaps that rough beginning caused him to be harder."

The next weekend Alma and Kenneth gave them a wedding party in their basement. "That's what you see in the photo," she said. "Right before the picture was taken I told your dad I wanted a divorce." She wore her white graduation dress. Her wedding dress was the gray skirt and green blouse she wore to work that day. There are no pictures of the wedding. Nor of the honeymoon, since they didn't have one.

This was not the story I had told myself. In my head, he carried her off to a road trip and a cottage. Mackinac Island on the Upper Peninsula or Traverse City during cherry season, hot cups of coffee in bed warming cold toes after hunting for Petoskey stones and morel mushrooms.

My mother paused and mumbled something I couldn't understand. James started down the stairs, then turned back. Maybe he saw in my face the transformation of my parents' wedding from a celebration to an accident. A mistake. A life-changing wrong turn.

"I tried to move back to the Y," my mother said. "But they wouldn't let me. Said I'd broken curfew. You're away the whole night and they call you a loose woman."

"Did you look for someplace else to stay?"

"I tried," she said. "By the time I found a place, I was already pregnant."

I wanted to hold my mother. I should have. I wished I could have pressed her head and plump, grandmotherly body against my chest, comforted her, told her everything was going to be all right, nurtured her the way her mother never did. But I could barely move.

Ella walked in, sweaty from basketball, and said, "Mommy, you look terrible." When I rubbed my eyes, I'd muddled my mascara.

James climbed downstairs. "We have to leave in five minutes!"

Ella ran to her room to put on a dress, and I hurried into the bathroom to change contacts. I looked at my ring, with my father's diamond in it, one of the only objects of his I own. I could now see so much more than I had noticed before. I imagined the wrapped-up box my father gave my mother for her eighteenth birthday. Inside, the ring she would wear around her neck and push under her blouse. I could see the secret she hid from her mentally unstable mother. I could see her ticket out of that unhealthy household. I could see her hand trembling, the weight of a diamond as heavy as a whole life, too much for a newly minted and unprepared eighteen-year-old.

Eighteen. The age of my about-to-graduate son. I couldn't imagine him marrying yet. I don't want him to have to grow up too fast, then think it is too late to change his mind, before he is even old enough to drink. I want him to have the time to live alone. To find out who he is and what he wants. I want him to have the equivalent of my mother's experience at the Y.

YOUNG WOMEN'S CHRISTIAN ASSOCIATION. No one calls it that anymore.

For me, the Y is swimming lessons for Noah on 9th Street in Brooklyn. The camp in Upstate New York, where he spent every summer since age eleven. The 92nd Street Y in Manhattan for speed dating and readings.

The song says, "You can stay there, and I'm sure you will find many ways to have a good time."

The Y is an empty container. My mother poured in her youth and left it there. Sometimes we can't go home.

"What a woman needs is her own money and a room of her own," Virginia Woolf said. If she can't have both, try for one. If my mother couldn't go back to the Y, at least she could get a job, after my father died.

At first my mother worked as church secretary. But Pastor Riddle said she was too young and blonde and pretty. People talked, the gossip filtering back to the rectory.

So she took a job typing for a company that printed ice cream bar wrappers, then a better job at the American Legion, which her second husband made her quit. After that brief marriage ended, she found a spot at the secretarial pool of a big bank Downtown. Not far from the Y.

My Y? I left my youth on 107th Street, between Broadway and Amsterdam. Right before college graduation, I found the share. Carol, a middle-aged single woman with a dog, lived in a large rent-controlled apartment and sought a roommate. The rent was cheap, the space a castle.

Like my mother, I left the place where I felt most myself. The only non-student home I lived in as an adult without a boyfriend, husband, or child.

My why? I had to keep asking.

MY PARENTS MARRIED IN 1964, not 1864. In America, not Afghanistan. Women could choose their partners and decide when—or even whether—to get married.

But I understand a little how my mother allowed herself to be rushed into a life-changing event she wasn't nearly ready for. How she could be swept up in the momentum of other people's desires. How she could find herself drawn to someone who pursued her. How she could say something, from the crazy place of "rebound" that would prove impossible to retract. How she would be haunted by regrets that she ever agreed to such a mismatch, knowing her husband might have been much happier—and kinder even, as a result—with a different wife.

I understand more than a little.

Because I did these same things myself.

I was twenty-two when my friend Lee Ann introduced me to Andrew. My college boyfriend had just dumped me and announced he was engaged to someone else. I learned from a mutual friend that he'd been cheating on me with other women too, the whole four years. I took some responsibility, of course. I must have been unable to see what was right in front of me. I didn't have much trust in my ability to choose men at that moment, so I let a friend pick one for me.

Lee Ann invited Andrew and me to her apartment for dinner that summer, cold ginger-carrot soup, grilled cheese, and microbrew. She lived on the Lower East Side of Manhattan in a shabby-genteel building, across the hall from the famous Beatnik poet Allen Ginsberg.

Andrew was a filmmaker, I was a poet, and Lee Ann was both, a bridge between our two worlds. She had a lilting North Carolina accent, hipster horn-rimmed glasses, retro dresses, and a sex kitten voice.

I adored her. Everyone did. She could flip her hair in such a fetching way that the guy behind the counter at Anthology Film Archives would offer her a free ticket, without even being asked.

Maybe I secretly wanted to be seduced by Lee Ann. Letting her match-make for me was the next best thing.

When I met him, Andrew was twenty-nine. He was tall and lanky, nerdy looking in suspenders, black canvas slippers from Chinatown, and black-rimmed glasses the color of his curly hair.

I was skinny and outfitted in mismatched thrift-store clothes not nearly as chic as I imagined they were. My voice was soft and shy. Only when I performed my poems at bars or the St. Mark's Poetry Project, where Lee Ann and I co-curated a series, did I bellow and project. Only then could people hear my "real" voice.

Lee Ann pulled out a 16mm projector and showed one of Andrew's short films, abstract and painterly, in the Maya Deren school. "Don't you think it's just like your poems?" she asked, the sizzle in her voice warming me to the man she'd placed beside me.

Lee Ann gave Andrew my phone number and he called to ask me out the next day. He sent me letters, handmade cards-as-artwork, drawings he'd made of me, and fussy little romantic presents like scented candles in the most exquisite wrapping paper I'd ever seen. I was too flattered by the attention to tell him I needed time alone, space between boyfriends, a room of my own.

So I let him shoot me. "I don't photograph well," I cautioned.

"That's because you need someone to film you through the filter of love."

Andrew was right. He knew how to make me beautiful in his films—silhouetted in shadows and slanted sunlight against windows, my face superimposed over lace curtains. My skin shimmered. All my blemishes disappeared. He turned me into a muse, immortalized. A Francophile, like me, he knew the way to win me over was to transform me, on screen, into the visual equivalent of a Rimbaud poem.

Just a few months after we met, he wanted me to move in with him. Maybe I said yes to avoid hurting his feelings. Maybe I was used to doing what people wanted me to. Maybe I was acting in the crazy way people do when they're on the rebound.

On one of our first dates, Andrew showed me the scar on his chest where he'd tried to kill himself with a razor. I was so young and naïve, I romanticized his pain as "artsy angst." And I was so uninformed, I thought I could cure him, with nothing more than love and kindness.

The scar on his chest. The scar on my father's stump, which he showed my mother right away. I don't know what to make of these parallel wounds, but if I close my eyes, I can feel them both, cutting into my skin.

I knew so little of mental illness. I thought every neurotic thing Andrew did (wearing "lucky" clothes, eating only certain foods, avoiding a street or a step, tapping furniture, and rewriting list after list "to be safe") was proof that he was a real artist. Not like me, the practical one, straightforward and competent in a midwestern way that had started to bore me. His "eccentricity" was proof, to me, that he lived in the clouds, up where I couldn't reach, in the place where art and epiphany were made. I was sure everyone found his "quirks" as charming as I did. Until a teacher diagnosed him.

I was barely out of college, working as an editor, when I took an evening children's writing class at the New School in the West Village. The teacher assigned us to write a character sketch of a person we knew. I wrote about Andrew and his "idiosyncratic" relationship to objects. How every day he would pick them up and place them down again, tapping them a precise number of times. How he'd know when I had rearranged a sheet of paper or a vase and how he'd "realign" a room when I'd "interfered" with its proper order. I thought my workshop would laugh at the colorful character I'd created on the page. Instead, the teacher said, "So you decided to write about an obsessive compulsive?"

I didn't even know what that term meant. I had to look it up in the dictionary.

WHEN I MET ANDREW I lived in "my Y," the shared, spacious, rent-controlled apartment on 107th Street between Broadway and Amsterdam I'd found through college housing listings. The woman seeking a roommate had lived in the apartment for decades, filling it with antiques and polishing the floors. When she'd moved in, the sidewalks were littered with heroin needles. When I arrived, the streets were clean, but the rent was still dirt cheap. All my friends envied me.

Why did I leave? I'd known Andrew only months before I let him convince me to give up my charming, quiet steal in Morn-

ingside Heights and move into his loud, roach-infested studio in a
tenement on the dicey part of the Lower East Side.

I want to shake the woman I was, like a salt shaker, like Shake
'n Bake chicken, like a Shaker chair, like a milkshake, like a cocktail.
I want to rattle some sense into her. But I also want to listen to that
girl-woman, to hear her story, the story I've really only been able to
understand after hearing my mother's.

IN THE MONTHS THAT FOLLOWED, Andrew's mental state declined. Not
only didn't I "cure" him, I made him worse. He had an MFA in film
and had been teaching in San Francisco, but now that he was in New
York, he took a minimum wage job at a bookstore. Most of the time
he arrived late. A quarter of the time he didn't arrive at all. Then that
quarter became a half. He was fired. Months later, he found another
job, but the same pattern repeated. After that he stopped looking.

I can't blame Andrew. He didn't force me to become the bread-
winner and housekeeper. I thought I was taking care of him, at the
expense of myself, because that's what you do when you're married.
That's how you showed you loved someone. You sacrificed yourself.
I'd vowed to stay with him, even in sickness. But what if being married to me was bad for his mental health?

Soon after we met, Andrew was offered a job as a film curator
in Los Angeles. I made plans to relocate with him. I was willing to
give up a job and friends I loved, the city I had yearned to live in all
my life, for him.

Later, plane tickets in hand, he turned the job down. He'd never
get on a plane again, he said. Didn't people know he had a panic
disorder? How could they expect him to fly?

He missed his brother's wedding because he wouldn't board a
plane. Then he wouldn't take cabs. Wouldn't drive. Wouldn't go
over bridges. I should have been wary. But I married him anyway.
Like my mother, I'd convinced myself it was too late to back out.

Finally, Andrew no longer left the house. He begged me to stop
attending social events. Anywhere I went, I had to go by myself.

I adopted a dog. But that wasn't enough. I had a baby.

It's hard to regret anything I did. If I hadn't married Andrew, I wouldn't have Noah. My mother says the same thing about her own first marriage: "I can't imagine not having you kids. I might have had some mean and nasty ones instead. Or worse, none at all."

I took editing jobs to work on after Noah fell asleep. I juggled freelance work with a full-time job to afford daycare for my son. Andrew couldn't tend him. "I'm an artist," he said. That phrase was supposed to explain everything: Why he couldn't work, why he needed to sleep erratically and late, why he couldn't be expected to follow my bourgeois norms and rules.

One day Andrew bought a new stereo system for $700, money we didn't have. I called my credit card company and removed his name from the account. That didn't stop him from spending all our cash on rare records, CDs, and hi-fi equipment.

He started calling me at work and urging me home. "Use your sick days," he said. "I'm sick with missing you."

"I love you," he wrote on flowery notes tucked into my briefcase. "You are my whole world. I am panicked and miserable when you're not here. You're my safe person, my angel. I need you. Come home."

These notes pulled me in. Like quicksand.

I don't want to blame Andrew. His panic disorder was real, like the mental illnesses of so many others I know, who struggle with pain every day. I wish I could have helped him.

Our landlords sold the brownstone we lived in, and the new owners raised the rent so much we could no longer afford our third-floor walk-up. We moved into an apartment in The Yellow House (as Noah still calls it), a tenement building with break-ins through the fire escape and drug dealers yelling at each other deep into the night above us. The paint peeled on the outside, the carpet on the stairs showed new cigarette ashes every morning, and the walls were so thin I could hear the emaciated insomniac above my bedroom threaten, when she heard my alarm go off, that she'd call *People's Court* on me—as if the TV show were her own private bouncer.

That apartment was my anti-YWCA. I looked at the unraveling carpet of the filthy brown stairs, and I saw myself.

Alma, the matriarch of the family, my father's mother, saved me. After she had a stroke that paralyzed one side, my grandfather took care of her, learning not just to cook but to bake and can and quilt. After he died, my Aunt Cora took on the herculean task of caring for Alma for the rest of her life. After Alma died, she took care of us, by putting all six grandchildren in her will.

That money saved me. It was enough to quit my extra freelance job, to find another apartment, to buy a car, and to file for divorce.

Once my grandmother was paralyzed, she couldn't talk. Only one word. And only if she sang. "Yes. Yes. Yes."

I like to imagine her, in the afterworld, baking cakes and making a dozen flavors of fudge. Always full of energy, the way she was in life. The woman who defied gender norms of her generation by getting a job after her children grew up. Who would send hundreds of Christmas cards, who won themed hat contests at the senior center, who volunteered at church, who picked gallon upon gallon of wild blackberries Up North and baked them into pies, who was always sewing quilts and crocheting afghans for all of her grandchildren. The family photographer and chronicler who later sent chatty letters and homemade snickerdoodles and fudge to my college dorm.

I see her smiling, laughing, cheering me on, as I take her money and run. Run away. Start my first steps toward becoming the strong, independent woman she was.

Her red hair flying, she opens her mouth to sing. "Yes! Yes! Yes!"

I USED MY GRANDMOTHER'S MONEY to vacate The Yellow House, to pay an instructor to teach me to drive, and to buy my first car. Noah and I lived in a small drug-dealer-free walk-up in Brooklyn. And I met James. The story I tell goes like this.

The nicest thing I own is the first thing you see when you walk into my house—a red, handmade rug purchased in Tehran, haggled over in Farsi and delivered, in person, to the Brooklyn apartment of the man who would become my husband.

Back then, James told me the woman who gave him the rug, a woman he had recently dated, was by then "just a friend."

I didn't believe men and women could be "just friends." At least not if they were single, with one or both actively seeking a romantic partner. Yet I also agreed to be "just friends" with James, at first.

I was the one who contacted him. We had both joined a dating service called, pretentiously enough, The Right Stuff, after seeing an ad for it in *The New Yorker*. "I liked your profile," he wrote in his first e-mail, "but didn't contact you because you have a child."

At least he didn't write, as several others had, "Thank you for being so honest."

It's a line that makes you ask yourself: How could a mother lie about being a mother? Not ethically, but logistically? Maybe a liar would wait until the man is smitten, then spring the child on him and shout, "Surprise!" But to what end?

I had tried to meet other single parents. I met a man who humble-bragged about the $10,000-a-month child support his ex-wife demanded for his daughters' clothing allowance. I met another who asked how much I weighed, as if I were a chicken and he was considering me for a recipe. Then there was the man who told me about his summer plans to share a house with other singles on Fire Island.

"Do you do that every year?" I asked.

He let out a puff of air. "Of course not. Next year I'll be married."

"Married to who?"

"I don't know yet." Meeting my eyes over his mojito, he said, "Maybe to you."

I also met plenty of nice men with whom I had nothing in common except similar philosophies on effective potty training. So when I saw the Right Stuff ad, I thought, "At least someone I meet through an ad in The New Yorker will be someone who reads The New Yorker, and we'd have that to talk about. Maybe I could find a man who reads the arts listings, and maybe even—if I could be this lucky—the poetry and fiction."

I did. He was JamesNYC125. I was RedWeather. He responded to my first e-mail, "A redheaded editor in Brooklyn—what could be better? But dating a woman with a child would be complicated, as I'm sure you know."

I did.

"Let's not date," he suggested. "Let's just get together as friends."

That summer we both had travel plans, so a whole month passed before our first date—or our first "playdate," I guess. In the meantime, we e-mailed every day. I sent him poems, he sent me music. Even while discussing academic publishing, from my side as an editor and his as a researcher, we couldn't help flirting.

An economist, he would answer a question with, "Probability of 1."

"I love it when you talk math talk," I'd say.

And he would reply, "I can do it any time you want."

Our first meeting was on Smith Street. We talked books, then strolled to BookCourt, slid a novel off the shelf, and read passages aloud. His timing was perfect, his voice what I'd hoped it would be from the e-mails.

"I'd love to walk with you on the promenade," he said, and then sneezed. "But I should nurse my cold."

I wanted to nurse his cold too. I wanted to boil him a pot of lemon-honey tea and kiss him. Later I did, leaning against a car parked at a meter outside an elementary school. We both pretended I hadn't.

The next morning, he called to ask me to a modern dance performance in two weeks. We both lived in Brooklyn but met, for the second time, in Manhattan. His hand grazed my thigh in the dark, a moment I would replay over and over in my head.

For our third non-date, I suggested attending a concert on a barge docked near the Brooklyn Heights Promenade. Our knees touched in our cozy seats two rows from the string quartet.

Next we hiked Bear Mountain. "I didn't think a skinny girl like you could outpace me," he said. Then later, "I'm only letting you walk ahead so I can get a good view of you from back here."

So I vamped my hips. When we removed our hiking boots and socks in the car, we stared at each other's naked feet.

Non-date No. 5 was dinner at my place. Back then the nicest thing I owned was also the first thing you saw when you entered: a red futon couch. I chose the cover from the remnants section of a fabric store on the Lower East Side. It was something I could unzip and clean whenever a child spit up, spilled Cheerios, or wiped peanut butter on it. When I pulled a book off the shelf to show James, the Pokémon cards I used for bookmarks fell out.

Later, we found ourselves in bed. Finally. And that's when he confessed, "I'm dating someone else." She was a fellow economist he had met at a conference around the same time he met me, an Iranian-American who lived in Washington, DC.

"Now you tell me?"

"You knew we could only be friends."

"You have sex with all your friends?" I removed his hand from my belly. "I bet she doesn't even know about me."

I told him we had to either date or not see each other again. We were both traveling for Thanksgiving, so we decided not to e-mail or phone until we returned home. Then he would call and tell me which woman he chose.

Somehow I had turned myself into a dating-show contestant, a real-life version of one of those *Bachelor* shows my friends watch.

I flew to Austin to share the holiday with my brother. "I've met the one," I said. "Just because it sounds corny doesn't mean it isn't true."

"Does he feel the same way?" my brother asked.

I asked myself that question from the time I woke up until the time I went to bed, and sometimes in the middle of the night too.

James and I had e-mailed every day for months, long letters detailing our whole lives. I kept checking my inbox in Austin, though I knew it would come up empty.

On the flight home, I tried to imagine my competitor. She grew up in the center of an ancient civilization. I grew up in Detroit.

Her furniture probably smelled like an exotic perfume, not peanut butter. She was not a single mother. James had already informed me about how complicated dating a single mother could be. Did I even have a chance?

Trying to think like a statistician, I put my odds a 50–50. Or, as an economist would say, probability 0.5.

Minutes after I arrived home, James called. "I choose you," he said. I dropped the phone and fell onto the bare floor.

Weeks later, he buzzed me up to his apartment. The door opened to reveal the most beautiful rug I had ever seen, so finely woven it was more like a tapestry. The kind of precious object that could be ruined by a few stray Cheerios crumbs.

"It's a gift from a friend," he explained. "She bought it when she visited her family in Iran."

"She's trying to get you back," I said.

"What? She's just being kind. Don't you love it?"

"Sure." I loved imagining what I would do to it after it collected enough dust. I'd take it outside, hang it upside-down, and beat it with a stick.

But James turned out to be right. Sometimes a rug is just a rug. And sometimes men and women can be friends, even after they have been romantically involved. Rug Woman never tried to win him back.

Time passed, and I asked James if he ever wished he had chosen her.

"No," he said. "You're perfect for me."

Right. I wasn't the kind of person who would fantasize about walloping an innocent inanimate object. At least I wasn't anymore.

Months later, James met my son, Noah. I cooked his favorite, "chicken with crumbs," and after our dessert of apple crisp we played Clue.

The next day, Noah asked, "Can I have another playdate with my new friend?"

"Which one?"

"James."

Now we share the rug. It holds a place of honor in the house James and I bought together. I vacuum it with care.

When Ella asks, as she frequently does at bedtime, "Tell the story of how you met Dad," I tell her this one, though the G-rated version. And then I add this.

One year after we met, sprawled across a bench, knees over knees, hips touching, hands in each other's pockets, skyscrapers in the distance, barges right below, twilit tourists and locals strolling past us on the Brooklyn Heights Promenade, we became engaged.

A year after that, we married.

A year after the wedding, we gave birth to you.

Sleep well. You need your strength to grow those aching legs that make you half-giraffe.

And when you seek out boys, then men, perhaps you'll be too wise to date one who says he can't date you. Maybe you won't be a single woman with a child. It did complicate things, didn't it? Perhaps you'll learn from my mistakes.

Or not. See in what felicity they've landed me. Here, beside your bed, your soft, sweet breath just like your dad's.

Your eyelids shut, whole paragraphs ago you drifted off. You dream of promenades and perfect Sunday afternoons. Or maybe of the boy in Spanish class, his nerdy glasses half askew. Will he be "the one"? Probability zero. Even I talk that way now.

Once James and I escaped from the "friend zone," we did much more than stare at each other's naked feet. But I'm not going to tell my daughter that part.

There are some things we don't need to know about our parents. Right?

A NEW HUSBAND, A NEW name. I transformed into a Harrigan, leaving no traces behind, no breadcrumb trail. My sense of direction was spotty, so I should have known I'd need every clue I could gather once it came time to wend my way back to the beginning of my story.

Part 3
Paris

Overleaf: "The signs were everywhere." Condom Man, August 2012

August 2012 to August 2013

SCANT MORE THAN A YEAR after I began looking for my father, I ran away from him again, as far from his haunts as I could wander. What's the opposite of Detroit? Paris.

James was offered a sabbatical and invited to teach for a year at a *Grand école*, the French equivalent of the Ivy League. Ella attended a French school and Noah remained in the States, moving to a college dorm, the first time on his own. Despite—or likely because of—his trash and bug essays, his first choice accepted him.

The signs were everywhere. We first spied them out the airport taxi window. "I Am Your Friend" claimed a giant pink cartoon, in several languages. "Look," I said to Ella, "how cute."

James elbowed me, then I saw: Our "friend" was a condom. King Kong size.

"What is he?" Ella asked. "A giant hotdog?"

"Hey!" I pointed out the window, "the *Tour Eiffel.*"

The next day we strolled past the poster again on block after block. "There's the funny hotdog man," she said. "Why is he everywhere?"

"It's a welcome to Paris sign. Just for you." That's the story I told.

Once set in motion, a story continues, on its own. Isn't that a law of physics?

She curled up her lip, then invented her own explanations, more plausible than mine. About how we should be friends with people even when they don't resemble us. Or just because someone's huge and weird looking doesn't mean he's not friendly. Soon it was too late to confess this pink freak was urging safe sex.

It's harder to untell than tell a story.

We crank out stories, sometimes, to correct mistakes. Or fill in blanks.

THE COLD, DAMP AIR HUNG in our bedroom, waking me in the middle of the night. I lay next to James, panting with exertion from this dream: I'm the dancer on stage in *An American in Paris*. This time, not only do I forget my lines, I blank out on the steps. I trip over my big toe and splat on my back. My swirly dress flips up and shows my underpants. The audience laughs because it's Thursday and my panties say "Wednesday."

"I WANT YOUR LIFE," MY American friends told me. They wished they could move to this fairy-tale city, where crunchy outside/airy inside bread, wine as old as the gods, and cheese as slippery and pungent as sex are subsidized and plentiful (and really, who needs more than those three things when those three things are perfect?) Where building façades, destroyed and recreated in the nineteenth century, flaunt their balanced symmetry. Where trees are trimmed to look like lollipops.

At a party before we left, my friend Pam, who likes to post photos of herself in a bikini on Facebook, asked if she and I could husband-swap, just for the year. I don't think she was kidding. I knew I lived in paradise. So did Odysseus, for seven seemingly interminable years.

BACK IN VIRGINIA, ELLA HAD said, "Tell me about Calypso."

"She was a goddess," I had replied. "Prettier and smarter than Penelope."

Ella had heard these stories time and again so she finished this one herself. "Odysseus could ask for anything. If he stayed with her, he'd never have to die. He could be a god."

"He didn't want that," I said.

"Why not?"

"Even if your friends and teachers are nice, even if they gave you a bag of Gummi bears that magically refilled whenever you finished, even if you could have a birthday party every day, would you want to stay at school forever?"

"No way." She clawed her hands around my belly.

"Exactly," I said. "You'd do anything to find your way home."

I JOINED A WEEKLY PARENT group at Ella's school in the fifteenth arrondissement. James did too, the first few weeks. We arrived at one member's building, in the tony sixteenth, near Trocadero, the Parisian equivalent of Central Park West. Pascale led us through her museum-disguised-as-apartment, then served coffee from a silver pot. She owned the whole floor, so much space even the pool table had a room (and maybe even money) of its own.

At the end of two hours, James and I exited the elaborately wrought iron elevator and spilled onto the avenue, the *Bateaux-Mouches* on the Seine gliding in the horizon. "You know that was a Picasso on the wall," he said. "And those African masks? That Modigliani?"

We lived in a walk-up with a kitchen described, by most who saw it, as the smallest kitchen they'd ever seen. I'd never been this rich. Anyone who can afford to live in Paris is rich, by my definition. I was rich enough to afford a state-subsidized public/private hybrid school. A school that, despite its inexpensive price tag, attracted celebrities, politicians, and (apparently) art collectors. But I could never invite these people over. I couldn't explain my carpet stains.

At Ella's class picnic on the Champs de Mars, the Tour Eiffel looming like a monster picture postcard, my Parisian friend Kelley described a party her older daughter attended. The birthday girl's parents, a Brazilian supermodel and a French high-ranking Google executive, hired waiters to serve hors d'oeuvres. Champagne flowed for fourteen-year-olds.

At the same picnic, my friend Jane told us about her son Dylan's school encounter with the daughter of the former president of Kazakhstan. "What do you want for your birthday?" the girl asked Dylan.

"A long board," he said. A kind of skateboard.

The next day the girl handed Dylan an envelope filled with 150 euros in cash. More than $200.

"What's this for?" he asked.

"I thought you wanted a long board," she said.

This was my milieu. All I could think of during my friends' anecdotes were the lyrics of a Loretta Lynn song. "I was born a coal miner's daughter."

I'd never wanted to eat greasy hamburger with macaroni, banana pudding with vanilla wafers, and Shake 'n Bake barbeque chicken legs as much as I did here. I'd never wanted to eat that at all, not after I left home at eighteen. Now I craved even fried bologna on Wonder Bread, which we used to balance on our knees in front of the TV as kids.

I grew up in a modest but adequate house. What made me the object of pity was losing my father. Poor child, people would say. Poor. I couldn't get that word out of my head.

I owned the most pathetic underwear of any woman in Paris. Not that I checked, it's just a guess. On my block almost every other store displayed racy panties. Lacy, dainty, frilly affairs, plus leather and leopard-skin prints. No wonder Parisian women are so thin. They spend their food money on bras. I told myself I didn't buy new bras because I was frugal. Maybe I was trying to prove it's not what's under the surface that counts. That no one could see through me.

Ella attended school with the children of the former French president. Chauffeurs dropped off the spawn of diplomats and actual princesses at the corner, and their bodyguards walked them to the entrance. Philippe, James's best friend and colleague in Paris, was asked to join the president's economic cabinet. When the most recent recipient of the best first novel prize in France invited me to lunch, James urged me to accept.

"He's just being polite," I said. "Because he's Philippe's partner."

"No, he adores you," James said. He reminded me how much Christophe had raved, in front of dinner guests, about a short story of mine that had recently won a prize.

"I know," I told James. But I thought, *Until he discovers who I really am.*

My father's daughter. Though I didn't yet know what that meant.

"SCYLLA, THE SIX-HEADED MONSTER, lives in a cave high up on a rocky cliff," Circe told Odysseus. "Her long necks will snap up six of your men, one in each mouth. But if you row hard, the rest of you will escape."

Sometimes you have to keep rowing, even if you lose someone in the process. Even a son. That's the story I told myself.

IN OUR SKYPE CONVERSATIONS (SOMETIMES weekly, sometimes daily) Noah complained. One late night for him, early morning for me, he said, "I have nowhere to go for fall break. Thanksgiving, either. I don't want to bum a ride from a friend and sleep on his couch. The dorms close down, the cafeterias too. You rented our house. Someone's sleeping in my bed."

"Goldilocks?" I asked.

"Very funny."

"You could always visit your dad."

"Our connection's breaking up," he said. "Gotta go."

"Bye." The connection was fine.

Andrew lived in Ann Arbor now, in a tiny apartment not far from his brother. A short plane ride from Noah's college. But it might as well have been the North Pole.

A few days later, Noah lugged his computer outside in the dark, far from his roommate's snores. He didn't bother to set up the camera, so I had to imagine a glimmer of stars, perhaps a quiet family of deer in the woods huddled beside the bike rack. "Are you there?" I asked.

Nothing. I was about to hang up and make a pot of coffee.

"I'm here," he said, his voice crumbling.

"Anything wrong?"

Then he said, "I'm homeless."

I recognized, in the raw strain of his voice, my own at his age. Not as a freshman but during my junior semester abroad.

I'D ANTICIPATED THAT TRIP EVERY day since my first stay in Europe, when I was fifteen and got a lucky break. Uncle Dennis, my mother's brother-in-law, was hosting an international exchange with my cousin Chris's basketball team. He was taking a group of middle school kids to Stockholm for a week, to stay with Swedish families and play against local teams. I wasn't an athlete. But he let me come anyway after my Aunt Mary, his wife, helped raise money for the trip. Mary and Dennis always seemed so cosmopolitan—eating flaming cheese at Greek Town, hosting high school students from Germany, and drinking red wine—I would have followed them anywhere. I stayed with Ulrike, a girl my age, in her high rise. We ate fish eggs from a tube on licorice-flavored bread for breakfast. I mastered the underground and started wearing fringed scarves and sleek black boots, instead of white sneakers and puffy sweaters. I came back from that trip convinced I was a European accidentally born in America.

My high school French teacher, Madame Hausermann, taught me that France equals high culture. She turned me on to Rimbaud, Baudelaire, and Verlaine. A world of symbols, senses, and synesthesia. In her classroom parties, we nibbled croissants and sipped Perrier, Debussy wafting in the bubbles. *Afternoon of a Faun.* When I finally arrived in Paris, for the first time, I was twenty. I had a financial aid check for $1,700 to cover six months—rent, food, textbooks, school supplies, and travel. Work study didn't follow me, and I couldn't work legally. My class schedule was too full to be an *au pair.* If I didn't find a black market job I'd run out of money before I could buy my ticket home.

I snagged a cheap maid's room for $250 a month (shared Turkish toilet down the hall, no shower) and found a few babysitting gigs through Joseph, a friend of a friend who taught at a private kindergarten where I interned. I wasn't earning enough, though I cut my hair (badly) and never set foot in a restaurant.

Then Joseph offered me a deal. Anne-Marie, a famous poet, sought a companion. The pay was room and board and even spending money. I'd won the lottery. The catch? I had to return by six and couldn't leave again till after dawn. Seven days a week. I was Cinderella with an earlier curfew.

Anne-Marie was "nervous"—that's how Joseph explained her need for company. I later learned the name of her condition—agoraphobia. From the Greek, meaning fear of open areas, fear of crowds. Panic that worsens when the person is alone or away from home.

I didn't yet know I was a magnet for agoraphobes. That soon I would marry an agoraphobic man.

When I first met Anne-Marie, in her apartment, she read my poetry and pronounced it "very American." "You have so many *things* in your poems," she said. "You Americans are so physical, so concrete. Why do you like objects so much?"

Followers made pilgrimages to visit her. Mysterious and haunting on the page and in person, her art was so theoretical, spare, and austere it almost disappeared.

She was a celebrated literary recluse, but she held court in her apartment in Neuilly-sur-Seine, on the outskirts of Paris, where I was often allowed to crash dinner parties with literary legends I was too young and naive to be as intimidated by as I would be now. In my memory, we served the same meal to everyone: an *entrée* of radishes, fromage blanc, and fresh herbs; lamb chops broiled with fresh rosemary for the *plat*; salad; strong, stinky, delicious, soft Muenster cheese; wine and bread, of course; coffee, and sometimes vodka at the very end. She didn't drink but liked to try to get me drunk. I wasn't sure what she enjoyed more—loosening up a seemingly straightlaced kid unused to liquor or living vicariously through me.

I HAD GONE TO PARIS thinking I was going to find my spiritual home, a land of people with whom I could finally fit in. But Anne-Marie made me feel more American than I ever had before. When I cooked myself roasted green peppers stuffed with rice or tomato sauce with tofu over whole wheat noodles, she said, "Is this what Americans eat? Army food?" When I dressed in flowered jeans and red cowboy boots, she asked, "Is it true, this is what they call fashion in your country?" When I trimmed my bangs (accidentally) crooked, she wanted to know, "This is what passes for American style?" It's hard to look stylish or to prepare elegant French recipes when you have no money. My vegetarianism also puzzled her—how could Americans be so perverse that they avoid all the best foods? Because Anne-Marie lived a life that was isolated in many ways, she saw me as a completely typical American, an attitude that molded my individual personality into a series of clichés. Or so it felt to an impressionable twenty-year-old, still struggling to see how she fit in the world. But I'm grateful to Anne-Marie, and to Joseph for finding her for me. Without them, I might not have been able to stay in Paris at all.

Now, decades later, I was back in France, the place that first taught me I couldn't pretend to be something I wasn't. The country

that revealed how American I was. The city that kept reminding me
I was so far from home.

IN DECEMBER, THE CHRISTMAS MARKETS turned the Champs-
Élysées into a festival of ice rinks and Ferris wheels, mulled wine
and incongruously hot beer. Ella was especially enamored by the
glass blowers. We spent half an hour ogling a fragile menagerie,
then cooing over snow globes with Parisian monuments inside.

They're so delicate. So easy to break. Their sharp shards could
shatter on the floor and pierce my bare soles.

I bought Ella a glass snail for Christmas instead.

OVER A HUNDRED YEARS AGO, in the storybook city of Vienna, a
surgeon asked a medical instrument maker named Erwin Perzy to
create extra-bright lighting for his operating room. Cobblers often
filled a globe with water and placed it before a candle to magnify
the light, so Perzy tried the same technique with an electric bulb.
To better the effect, he filled the globe with tinsel then white grit,
reflecting the bulb's light. As soon as the particles sunk to the bottom, though, the added brightness vanished.

Yet the effect of the white grit was magical. Like falling snow.

Perzy created a miniature church and placed it inside the globe,
with water and white grit. The snow globe was born.

When I was tiny, I thought the snow was real, that the globe
kept it frozen. Sometimes at night I dreamed I swam in the Snow
Globe Sea. I could enter its frosty kingdom by closing my eyes, and
I could be queen. If it broke, I was sure the flakes would melt. The
queen, like a creature of snow, might die.

But the snow globe wasn't made of snow. It was born of grit and accident. I didn't want to know that, so soon. To find out, at five, when my father boomed, "You didn't clean up your room" and broke every treasure on my dresser, that I wasn't actually a queen. The snow globe was supposed to be a medical advance, a scientific boon. Instead, it was a failed experiment. A botched invention.

NOT LONG BEFORE CHRISTMAS, I opened the *New York Times* and read on my screen, "Hundreds of terrified parents arrived as their sobbing children were led out of the Sandy Hook Elementary School in a wooded corner of Newtown, Connecticut."

Twenty-eight dead, most of them elementary school children like my daughter. The killer had access to semi-automatic guns, which his mother owned and kept in easy reach.

The next day, Ella and I undressed in the locker room of our local yoga studio right before our Saturday class. Half a dozen women, including my instructor, greeted me with this: "I'm so sorry. For you." They made the massacre sound like my personal tragedy.

I wanted to explain, No, *I'm* sorry we let this happen. We Americans. Instead, I hung my head and said, "It's so terrible."

After class, I removed my sports bra and stood naked in the middle of the locker room. "Why?" the women asked me now. "Why do you let people have so many guns?"

Me? I'm the one always signing gun-control petitions. I didn't say that, though. Instead, I told myself these French women were right. Guns are my heritage, part of where I'm from, even if I've never owned one. I thought we all absorbed the collective crimes of our countries, deciding to be proud or ashamed of ourselves, depending on what our fellow citizens did. Or our family.

The French women used the plural "you," meaning, "you people," all of you. It took so much energy to articulate my defense, to find the vocabulary in French, that I couldn't even pull on my loose-elastic, faded, cheap underwear, unlike the women around me who were already inside their smart Parisian outfits. Goosebumps crawled up my back.

My instructor looked at my chipped toenails. Or maybe she was just averting her eyes from my naked inability to explain.

I MIGHT TRACE MY INSECURITY back to Anne-Marie, when I translated her "so American" as "too unsophisticated to live in the most civilized city in the world," though I don't blame her for my mistranslation. Or maybe back to when I lost my father. When I became a member of the Creepy Club.

How many of us are there? People who say, "The thing about me you need to know is I lost my father young."

I can spot them easily now. They're the ones who let everyone pass them in the merge lane. They totter on stools, one foot in this world, one in another. They hover at the periphery of dinner party conversations, trying to shrink so small they may disappear.

Since I've learned what to look for, I've found quite a few. As a child, I thought I was the only one.

We're half-orphans, half-everything, living half a life. Fatherless children who, even after we grow up, continue to think of ourselves as fatherless children.

When my friend, whose father died when she was little, told me about her grandmother's recent passing, the frayed edges of her laugh reminded me she's one of us. "I wouldn't laugh in front of anyone else," she said. "But you understand. You *know*." I know what we both learned as children. That it is absurd for a grandparent to outlive a parent. That every breath we take brings us closer to reuniting with the men who, by dying so young, have become, in our perpetually childish imaginations, martyrs or even gods. Mysterious, frightening, and all-powerful. We keep looking for them, wherever they are. Sometimes they seem right next to us.

Something primal about our premature knowing makes us different from everyone else. Our lives seem more precarious. Even undeserved. When we memorize the facts of death before our multiplication tables, we can't unlearn those lessons any more than we can forget the product of three times three.

We are the ones with imaginary friends who are ghosts, who walk hand in hand with zombies and mummies. Death is our constant companion, while we jump rope and swing and whoosh down the slide. Our playmate, our best friend, our worst enemy. We nurse our notions of mortality the way other children might obsess with upcoming birthdays and trips to Disney World.

Sometimes we creep our classmates out when we tell them we wonder who will take care of us when our mother is gone. It doesn't occur to us she'll live till we grow up.

I want to hug these children, who are now adults. I want to tell them they're not alone. I know why they have a wicked, even morbid sense of humor. I understand their reasons for redirecting attention away from themselves. Why they think they're always coming up short, that everyone can see they have a missing a piece. Why they laugh, like my friend, when most people would cry.

I didn't know any other children without fathers when I was growing up. Any other members of my Creepy Club.

Except Jenny.

FROM THE TIME I WAS four till junior high, Jenny and I idled away long summer days squirting her shepherd-lab mix with the hose, then spraying each other's cut-offs and glittery painted toes. We crammed weekends full of Barbie-Ken strip teases on her porch, under a blanket-and-card-table fort. We played the Game of Life, my favorite, and when it was her turn to choose the activity, we listened to 45s on full blast, over and over, so we could scribble the lyrics to memorize and sing in the backyard, her dog barking as back-up.

Jenny and I were left largely unsupervised at her house while her mother worked on the assembly line at the Frito-Lay factory. Doubled up on her banana seat bike, Jenny and I rode to the candy store and bought malted milk balls and sugar cigarettes, showing off how we could balance with no hands. We whipped up mayonnaise on bread, with a smidge of tuna fish, in her cramped kitchen, washing down lunch with stashes of Cheeto snack packs that her mother got for free.

Four years my senior, Jenny was an unlikely best friend. Her father wasn't dead, but I don't remember ever meeting him. He was just "not around."

In my memory, my mother was "not around" much either, but that wasn't true. I told people she worked "all the time." But what I meant was that my siblings and I were on our own for hours every day, that she didn't return till after six o'clock, that our house seemed empty without her.

Soon after my father's death, my mother took a full-time typing job. Our elementary school had no cafeteria, so children walked home for lunch. My brother, sister, and I wore our house keys strung with yarn around our necks and took turns cooking canned chicken noodle soup and fried bologna on Wonder Bread at noon. We watched *Popeye* and *Wheel of Fortune* and *Road Runner* (my favorite), bowls of broth and plates of pink grease see-sawing against our thighs as we slouched before the TV.

When we forgot our keys, we camped out on the bench swing in the backyard, our beagle Ex on our laps. Fallen pears from the tree served as our lunch, unless our neighbor Mrs. Vann was home and lent us the key she kept just in case.

Mrs. Vann was the kind of woman who went to the hairdresser every week. My father used to poke fun at how immaculate she kept her house. She was also sickly and frail, often unable to rise from bed, so we tried to fend for ourselves.

How did Jenny feel about being left behind? We must have talked about it. I don't know if her parents were divorced or never married.

If her mother even knew who her father was. Did she think she was lucky that he didn't die? Or that I was lucky one, since mine didn't *choose* to leave me? It's too late to ask. I don't know where she's gone.

It's only now, as I walk the streets of Paris remembering my best friend, that my own answer surfaces. I was lucky to have a father who loved me beyond measure. If he didn't, he wouldn't have labored so hard to provide a home, safe and comfortable, for me and my family. He worked himself ragged. For what? For us.

I was lucky to have a father who was proud of his children. He loved to show us off to guests, asking us to sing.

"There were ten in the bed and the little one said, Roll over! Roll over! Then they all rolled over and one fell out." Plop! We acted out the scene. Our audience laughed. Our father beamed. We were headed for Broadway, you might have thought, from the wideness of his grin.

How could I have thought he never smiled? I climbed into the Metro to pick up Ella from school and finally remembered.

The song ended, "There was one in the bed and the little one said, 'Good night.' " We pretended to sleep.

On the train, our car climbed above ground. The Eiffel Tower hovered above. My breath slowed down, every muscle relaxed into a daydream, as I sang the song in my head and closed my eyes.

THAT NOVEMBER, WE VOTED IN the presidential election by absentee ballots. Shakespeare & Company, the storied American bookstore on the bank of the Seine, in the shade of Notre Dame, hosted a get-out-the-vote campaign, complete with a realistic young Bob Dylan impersonator strumming and singing rousing protest songs with a gravelly voice. I was eager to vote for Barack Obama a second time. My fellow citizens did the same, in record numbers. This time I absorbed the collective pride, not shame, of my countrymen and women.

The next day, I met Ella's best friend and her grandparents at a museum to see an exhibit on robots. The five of us—two kids, three adults—sat at the museum café drinking coffee and chatting in French. "I stayed up till 3 a.m. to follow the results," the grandfather told me.

I said I was impressed.

"It matters a lot who is going to lead the most powerful country in the world," he explained.

My country was strong, which meant I was too. Wasn't everyone this kind of chameleon?

My shoulders widened with his words. I sat up straighter. I could have sworn my biceps bulged.

NOAH FINALLY VISITED FOR CHRISTMAS break. He and I had spent months in different countries, talking in the middle of the night, repeating conversations like this.

Noah: I have a test tomorrow. I'm worried I'm going to bomb.

Me: Did you study?

Noah: Of course! That's not why I called. I just want you to tell me I'll do fine and everything will be OK so I can go to sleep.

Me: You're having insomnia? Did you listen to those sleep podcasts I e-mailed you?

Noah: That's not what I need. I don't want you to fix my problems. I just want you to tell me what I told you to tell me.

Me: Which is what?

Noah: That everything's going to be OK.

Me: It is. You know that. Do you need me to send you earplugs? Is it too loud to sleep?

Noah: Mom! Just say it.

Me: Oh. You just want me to say everything will be OK?

Noah: Yes!

Me: Everything will be OK.

Noah: Love you. Goodnight.

Me: Love you too. (By the time I'd said that, though, he'd probably already hung up. On his way to falling asleep, I hoped.)

Now we were together. My disembodied voice pinging across the ocean always sounded so puny on the phone. Finally, I could mother him.

We sat in the living room of our second-floor walk-up across from the Catacombs, drinking coffee after James and Ella left for work and school.

Noah, six-foot-two, with a jungle of gelled hair, a tattoo on his arm that reads "The Good, The Bad, and The Ugly" in Italian, and a black goatee, blinked and jiggled his leg, nervous tics since elementary school, and sprawled the length of one couch in his favorite thrift store clothes: Pac-Man fluorescent socks, skateboard shoes, a lumberjack flannel shirt, and Kung-Fu Panda cap worn backwards and askew. He seemed to take up the whole apartment.

I huddled on one small square of the other couch in my Parisian uniform—skinny jeans, cotton scarf, and black heels, low enough to be considered walking shoes here but high enough to seem fancy anywhere else. The windows looked onto the courtyard and rooftop flower garden. Light filtered through gauzy curtains, bleeding outlines of the florid ironwork on the railing.

"How's your anxiety?" I asked. This is a topic Noah and I discussed often, in the context of specific triggers. He paused a long time.

"I can't separate my anxiety from who I am," he said. "It's just a part of me." He picked at his fingernails. "How would you feel if I asked, How's your low self-esteem today?"

Tears came, despite my efforts to keep face, to show that I could help him deal with *his* issues. That I was the strong one, the solid wall he could lean on, the indestructible parent. I exhaled, trying to let go of more than my breath. "How do you know I have low self-esteem?"

"I didn't mean to make you cry," he said, moving off his couch onto mine, "but it's obvious, isn't it? You say the food you cook isn't good enough, that you're always taking the wrong train, walking or driving in the wrong direction. You're self-deprecating, not in a stand-up comic way either. You mean it."

I'd hoped I had done a better job of hiding my self-doubts, my certainty of nothing except that I didn't deserve the life in Paris everyone seemed to envy.

That I didn't deserve, perhaps, to still be alive. My father was dead at thirty-two. What was I doing, living into my forties? I didn't ride in the Jeep with him on his last night, as my sister did, but perhaps I had survivor's guilt too.

"If there's a piece of burnt meat on a plate, it's the one you choose," Noah said, "so nobody else will have to. If we're short an umbrella, you start claiming you like getting cold and wet."

"You shouldn't be raised by such a self-effacing mother."

"See?" he said. "See what you're doing?"

"What?"

He unwrapped a stick of gum and wadded it into his mouth. "You can't see?"

Now I realize what he meant. I couldn't even talk about my own self-growth without turning it into how I could help someone else.

BEGINNING IN COLLEGE, WHENEVER I met new people, they'd ask me what my father did for a living. The parents of my friends, especially, when they invited me over for dinner. It wasn't just small talk, I thought, but a way to place me. To put me in my place. When I said, "He's dead," they chewed their food silently. I imagined them thinking they didn't send their kid to a fancy school so she could become friends with orphans.

My mother's mother emigrated north from Appalachia to find a better paying job as a laundress. Her father moved from Missouri to be a security guard. My father's family farmed. We are unpretentious folk. So what was I doing here pretending? Crashing the party of the *Bourgeoisie*?

JANUARY WAS THE SEASON OF GAY marriage. *Mariage pour tous,* marriage for all, was the slogan.

We gathered at Denfert-Rochereau, the protest march capital of Paris, which also happened to be my neighborhood, waiting for the march to begin. Ella carried her sign high above her head, its stars and swirls spelling, in French, "We children support marriage for all." I carried mine, substituting "heterosexuals" for "children." James came too, his chants interrupted by sneezes.

We were mobbed by men and women asking to photograph us with our signs. Others thanked us as they walked by. Two women asked if they could hug us. It felt as if we were all part of history, the movement toward a better and more inclusive society. A future free from shame. And full of pride. James struggled to hold back tears almost as much as I did.

Man or woman, gay or straight, let us marry whomever we want. That's what the signs and chants said that day.

We should be permitted to couple and make our partnership official. We should also allow ourselves not to. We should not be rushed when we're not ready. Nor should we be stuck with someone who needs to be free.

I marched past the lion to the Jardin du Luxembourg, then to Les Halles, grateful for my own freedom. To choose a mismatch the first time. And then, once I knew more of the world and myself, to find "the one." I swayed my sign and sang for miles, clacking my ridiculous French heels (just like every other Parisian woman), under the perpetual rain, which plopped on my cheeks in drops as fat as tears. Thinking about my mother, who did have another chance at happiness. And my father. Who didn't get a second shot. With anything.

A FEW DAYS AFTER THE march, James's mother Tricia called. She never phoned without e-mailing first. This could mean only one thing.

"It's Bob," she said. Of course. James's father. "He's been in an accident." Bob was still alive; I could hear that information seeping through the phone.

"When are we flying back to see him?" I asked James.

"Not yet."

"Why not?" Last-minute flights from Paris to California would cost thousands of dollars. But this was his father.

"My dad's going to be OK," James said.

People today wear seatbelts and buy cars with airbags. Bob was bruised and shaken up, and the car would need to be totaled, but he was safe. Some people crash cars and walk out of the hospital, I realized. Bob would be released just days later.

Two of James's brothers, and seven of their children, visited us in Paris that spring. "Why don't I ever see my cousins on *your* side?" Ella asked me one weekend morning, while the rest of the apartment slept—James in our bed, his brother and sister-in-law in the guest room, his niece in Ella's room, and two nieces on a couch and foldaway bed. Ella and I huddled in our galley kitchen, preparing coffee and *chocolat chaud.* I opened the window onto the courtyard, the smell of rosemary and lavender wafting up to us.

"Uncle Lou doesn't have kids," I said. He and his wife, on their return trip from Florence to Austin at the end of the summer, were our first visitors here.

Ella drank her full-bodied, not-too-sweet French hot chocolate, browning her upper lip. "What about your sister?"

"She has kids, but she doesn't want to see me."

I stared down at my feet and mumbled, the way my mother sometimes does. Maybe I offered a cryptic response, something about a missing shoe.

"What?" Ella edged closer to hear better.

"I said put on your shoes. Let's surprise your cousins. How many croissants should we buy? Do you think they would like *pain au lait?*"

So MANY TIMES I WONDERED why my mother had allowed my sister to erase me. If she had just intervened, I reasoned, she could have at least forced Lynn to acknowledge my existence. She could have said, "Contact Sharon or else."

As if it were that easy.

I sat down at my computer and read a string of e-mails Andrew had sent while I was asleep. "Can you get Noah to return my calls?"

"Contact Andrew or else." I couldn't say that to Noah. Or else what?

I couldn't force my son to write back to his father, to return his calls, to respond to his texts. I wasn't even sure I wanted to. Would that be ethical? We have to be ready before we can engage in intimate relationships. The timing has to be right. Now I knew, for the first time, how my mother must have felt, caught in the middle.

I was editing a manuscript from a writer who cut herself off from her mother, the subject of her memoir. I was beginning to grasp how someone could do such a thing. This daughter needed time to see herself more directly, in a way that wasn't just a reflection of her mother's opinion of her.

Another book arrived in my in-box for editing, this time an autobiographical novel about a daughter who stopped talking to her mother. The writer prefaced the book by telling me we live in an era of estrangement. So many celebrities have cut ties with a parent. Angelina Jolie, Macaulay Culkin, Tatum O'Neal, and Kate Hudson, to name a few. But no one talks about it. There's too much shame, on both sides—the ones cut off and the ones doing the cutting. Maybe if we all started to share our stories, the shame might disappear.

For so many years I'd held onto a resentment against my mother for not convincing my sister to talk to me again. For letting my sister "get away with" her fatwa. What kind of magical thinking had I engaged in, imagining my mother had so much power? That any of us did?

My mother arrived in May.

"I always wanted to see Paris," she had responded, when I asked if we should buy her a ticket.

She'd always wanted to see Paris? I'd never heard that before. Certainly not when I lived here decades ago (when, to be fair, neither of us could have afforded her ticket). I'd always considered her uninterested in the world outside Michigan. Again, I'd read her wrong.

Her first time abroad was a trip with me to visit Louis in Italy. I was in my twenties. Noah was a toddler, and I left him with Andrew who, even that early in our marriage, refused to travel, not just in planes but in trains and buses and even sometimes in cars. When I was in premature labor with Noah, my water already broken and contractions in full swing, I had to take myself to the hospital because he was phobic of bridges and tunnels.

On that transatlantic trip, smoking was still allowed on planes, and my mother had not yet quit. She lit cigarette after cigarette. I still associate Europe with that smell.

Finally, in her sixties, she made it to Paris. One of the first things she wanted to see was where I'd lived, back when I came for my junior semester abroad. So we went on a pilgrimage to find my maid's room, the cheap place I found before the even cheaper place I shared with Anne-Marie. I didn't remember the exact address, just rue de Lille, in view of the Musée d'Orsay, on the left bank of the Seine. We rode the Métro there one morning. Rue de Lille is a short street with only about a dozen buildings. It's a fancy address that belies the modesty of its seventh-floor converted servants' quarters. The buildings protrude their grand, symmetrical, *Belle Époque* façades, their ornamental balconies bursting with window boxes, their concierges within, their courtyards protecting them from the vulgar noise of the street.

Each façade looks the same—like, well, a façade. Who could tell what lurked on the other side? I picked one, number eleven. "That's where I lived." A guess.

My mother wanted to take my picture. I scooted to the front of the courtyard door, hefty and florid. Snap.

"I always wanted to see where you lived," she said.

"You did?" I'd assumed, back then, her silence equaled apathy. I wish she had told me. I wish I had asked.

THE NEXT DAY WE TOURISTED the Louvre. On Sunday mornings, James, Ella, and I usually arrived at opening time and stayed till lunch. But on my weekday trip with just my mother, we arrived late in the morning and hit The Highlights. The Mona Lisa, cordoned off like a crime scene, covered with swaths of paparazzi. The Venus de Milo, the body of a giantess, each breast as large as my head.

"You know the story about Uncle Barry taking me out on a date?" my mother asked as we made our way through the crowds.

"I don't remember."

"I'm sure Barry's told you," she said. "He tells everybody."

"Tell me again."

We strolled past groups of Germans, Swedes, and Japanese, their guides holding up flags and talking into microphones that fed earbuds.

We walked through The Orientalist school of nudes in harems. Odalisques, reclining on daybeds, their necks supernaturally long, their breasts gleaming white and ripe as a Camembert. I forgot about the date.

My mother did not. "The three of you were little," she finally said, once we found seats on the benches and the crowds cleared for lunch. "After Barry got back from Vietnam, he came over one night and said to your dad, 'Jerry, you never take your wife out. She needs to go on a date. I'll watch the kids.' Your dad said, 'I'm too tired. You take her.' You know where Barry took me? Out on Dix, one of those X-rated places."

"A strip club?"

"They weren't completely naked."

"He took you to a topless bar?"

"Of course he picked front-row seats." She dropped her face in her hands, maybe the way she had at the bar. "I thought I'd die. But he meant well. He thought it was funny."

I didn't ask why she had been embarrassed. I'd felt the same way when a boyfriend took me to Hooters and the servers' breasts, popping out of push-up bras, practically landed on my plate. Though I don't think of myself as a prude. Or my mother, either.

I'M GRATEFUL, IN FACT, THAT my childhood memories are full of hints that sex between consenting adults was nothing to be ashamed of. I remember lying in bed, half asleep, hearing the mattress squeak in the room across from mine.

Then, much later, I remember my mother's boyfriends. Bob the Armenian mailman was my favorite. We often tagged along for our mother's dates at Bob's apartment, lingering in the living room, eating Little Caesar's and watching *Three's Company* while they sequestered themselves in the bedroom. I didn't wonder too much what they did. I inferred it was something that gave them pleasure, so it made me happy too.

CROWDS CONVERGED AT THE LOUVRE, but they spoke different languages, so we had the false impression no one could understand us. A tour guide with a Japanese flag led her group to the next room, and we breathed extra oxygen from the air.

My mother sat on her hands to warm them on the museum bench. I laid mine on the back of my neck.

"You have to understand," she said. "Lots of people went to topless bars back then. Things were different."

"I know." But I didn't really. I was a child in the early seventies. I hadn't even seen *Mad Men*.

"The way men thought of women," she said. "You can't judge people now for doing what was normal for back then. The same goes for your dad."

Of course. Lately, the conversation always returned to him.

"People today would call your dad a male chauvinist. But that wouldn't be fair. Because he wasn't."

She slumped, her sneakers tucked under her seat, next to my boots. "You're lucky to grow up when you did. When I was young, it seemed like people thought if a man changed a diaper, he'd grow breasts."

I laughed so hard I started to hiccup.

"So I should give Dad some slack?" I sucked in my lips. I didn't want to be unkind.

She jiggled her foot. "He was a man of his time."

I wasn't sure what that meant. Not all the men of that generation adhered to strict gender roles. I knew plenty who didn't, like my first boss after college, who treated me with more respect than I treated myself. Like Uncle Barry, who argued with a fellow worker who felt his daughter should marry instead of attending college like she wanted. Barry told him girls should be allowed to get an education so they can take care of themselves without depending on a man. If my father's refusal to give my mother access to a bank account or to pay for her clothes just made him "a man of his time," what about men like my uncles, who didn't view women as less important than they were? Didn't they belong to that time too?

Perhaps what my mother really meant was that I shouldn't pass judgment on a person until I considered the context. The world he lived in, the world I was trying to imagine.

WE LEFT THE MUSEUM AND boarded the train to the fourteenth arrondissement. Back home. In my mind, decades back. Circa mid-sixties to seventies, the era of my parents' wedding until my father's funeral.

Back then, clergymen told women their roles were divinely assigned. The most famous, Billy Graham, "saved" me at ten, when I knelt on the concrete floor of my football stadium seat and prayed, hoping to be born again among thousands. Graham wrote in the *Ladies' Home Journal* that women should bow down to their husbands too.

Men of that time liked their women weak. When *Ladies' Home Journal* asked two writers, male and female, "Do Strong Women Frighten Men?" both answered yes, adding, "As more and more women enter the workforce, men are finding a frightening new challenge to their jobs and futures: a whole new crop of ambitious and serious people—women. Added to this new competition, men now have to wrestle with their conditioned feelings that the people they're forced to compete with are, well, inferior."

How many generations will it take for that last word to go away?

Men at that time were used to having their wives ask for permission, like children. By 1974 (the year my father died), norms were starting to change (but by that time, it was too late for him). McGraw-Hill, the country's largest textbook publisher, advised its eight thousand authors and editors against statements such as, "Jim Weiss allows his wife to work part time." Instead, they should say, "Mrs. Weiss works part time."

Men flocked to X-rated movies. *Deep Throat* was a 1972 sensation. Censorship laws were struck down, and sex districts flourished in cities.

My father fit right in. Sexist? Nobody even used that word.

A 1971 shoe ad shouts at the top, "Attention male chauvinist pigs." Below four chunky-heeled, two-toned lace-ups, the smaller text reads, "Relax. When the 'Libs' call us names like that it really means we're rugged, masculine, virile."

A vermouth ad says, "What a catch! Martini & Rossi for cocktails that purr." A man in safari gear smirks at the blonde in a barely-there leopard skin sheath, captured in a cage. Two martinis tantalize outside the bars, beyond her reach.

In a coffee ad, a man with his back to us splays a woman across his lap, bottom up. Her face strains, his arm reaches up, ready to spank. Female readers are warned, "If your husband ever finds out you're not store-testing coffee . . . woe be unto you!"

A naked woman sidles on the floor, cheek pillowed on forearm. She stares, in awe, at a man's shoe. The text reads, "Keep her where she belongs." At your feet. Where you can step on her. Where she can worship you.

"It's nice to have a girl around the house." Under a picture of a man stepping on an animal rug with a woman's live face, the smaller text reads, "Though she was a tiger lady, our hero didn't have to fire a shot to floor her. After one look at his Mr. Leggs slacks, she was ready to have him walk all over her."

Even men who championed equal rights were men of their time. Reverend Martin Luther King Jr., father of the civil rights movement, did not allow women to perform the same jobs as men in his marches and ministry. Like Thomas Jefferson, not all great men were perfect. How could I expect my father to be?

Richard Nixon was a man of this time. John F. Kennedy. Lyndon Johnson. Gerald Ford. James Bond. Robert De Niro. Elvis Presley. John Wayne. Archie Bunker, the sit-com bigot who held court from his armchair. Meathead, Archie's lefty intellectual son-in-law too. The Six Million Dollar Man, part human, part robot. John Lennon. Malcolm X. Muhammad Ali. Andy Warhol. Woody Allen. Some of these things are not like the others. Some men were mavericks, but not, apparently, my father.

And the women?

Reader's Digest offered advice for the working woman on "How to Support Your Husband's Ego." She should avoid making him feel "inadequate by flaunting her own contribution to the family income."

My mother probably knew many other women without access to money. Before 1975, it was often impossible for a married woman to obtain a credit card or a loan without her husband's written permission. A 1970 article in *Time* magazine said, "Women are still depicted in many ads as scatterbrained homebodies, barely able to cope with piles of soiled laundry, dirty sinks, and other mundane minutiae."

SEX STILL SELLS, OF COURSE, even in the new millennium. But around me in Paris, I sensed a more equal opportunity sensuality.

Heading home from the Louvre with my mother, I caught out the Métro window two billboards facing each other on opposite sides of the platform, an ad I'd seen many times. Naked Handbag Babe filled the vast space with her smooth skin and svelte belly. She wore nothing and held a small leather sac in front of her vagina. The only text: 500 Euros. Across from her, Naked Perfume Hunk lounged on a polar bear rug, wearing only a blue-and-white striped scarf over one shoulder. One hand pressed the ice, which melted with his animal heat. A large perfume bottle, shaped like a male torso with a conspicuous bulge, obscured the part of his anatomy that, were it hung in the Louvre, might be covered by a fig leaf.

We passed another station and I saw on the platform one of the many online dating ads for extra-marital affairs. This one read, "It's six o'clock, do you know where your wife is?" It took me a while to understand the implication that must have been obvious to the French: She's having sex with someone else. Why shouldn't you?

Inside the train, an ad for the Natural History Museum showed gorillas in the act. The unwritten message of the picture was this: Take your children to an exhibit about animals and sex. There's nothing dirty about it. It's family fare.

American ads are not quite this explicit. Not anymore. My daughter gradually got used to the bombardment of naked images, but my nieces were shocked. These ads were of their time *and* place. And so, I suppose, were we: my father, my mother, and me.

Maybe I wasn't the only Gen X woman who imagined she wore the most pathetic underwear—anywhere. Maybe others hoped too that skipping lunch would Pygmalion them into cigarette-thin Parisiennes. Maybe they fretted they couldn't invite friends with fabulous apartments to their own humble homes. Perhaps others primped for the gym and refused to buy themselves new clothes or even panties till they "deserved" them. Maybe they prepared multi-course meals, ready the precise moment their husbands arrived and hesitated, as I did, to flaunt their superior language skills, ceding the spotlight to their husbands instead.

Will my children look back, decades from now, and try to forgive my anachronisms by telling themselves I came of age in another era? Will they explain away my my insecurity and overeagerness to please by saying, What do you expect? Hers was the first generation after women's emancipation? There are always growing pains. Learning curves.

I should have been relieved to learn my father was normal. But I had secretly wished he was *more* than a man of his time. If he could be singular, so could I. We could have both fallen from the sky.

Instead, he was an artifact of a time and place that's lost. Other men, other fathers of friends, have morphed into '80s men, '90s men, millennium men, and beyond. My father remains unchanged, like a figure enclosed in a snow globe.

What about me? I don't have to embrace the stereotypes of my gender. Maybe I don't have to run away from my father. I could steal some of his manliness for myself.

He'd love the Naked Handbag Babe. He'd cackle at Perfume Hunk the size of a *T. rex*. He'd slap his knee then pat me on the back when he saw the King-Kong-sized Condom Man, his poster blanketing every block. I wished my father were here to laugh at them—and ourselves—with me.

ONE SATURDAY, JAMES, ELLA, my mother, and I strolled through the Champs de Mars. It's probably the most crowded tourist area of a crowded tourist city, the place where it's most important to stay on guard.

But it was impossible to worry about anything on such an idyllic day. The May sun streamed down, ricocheted off the gleaming tower, and gushed over the lush green lawns, making up for the interminable rainy days we'd endured all spring. We had just picnicked on the grass and were full of baguette and Camembert. It was the kind of day you want to bottle and take back with you to the States, a souvenir of all this *belle ville* has to offer.

We strolled past an Indian family on the lawn eating sandwiches from Carrefour. A group of tall, blond, college students singing in Swedish. A barefooted Italian couple kissing on tiptoe. Two men performing an impromptu magic show.

The crowds thickened. We couldn't walk four abreast anymore. We huddled together, tried not to lose each other. I felt someone reach for my hand, then returned the affectionate gesture. Ella and James often grabbed hold of me while walking. But this hand felt different. Was it my mother's?

I swiveled to look. Then I screamed.

James shielded Ella with his body. My mother turned white.

At first all I saw behind me was a stranger's face covered by a scary Halloween mask of a witch—warts, hooked nose, broken teeth. I jerked my hand away as if yanking it from a fire. My scream made the masked man scatter, probably to hide behind a bush. His face was a flash of rubber and then it was gone. We quickened our pace, leaving behind the crowds lining up to scale the tower.

Only later did I realize "the hand" had been after my diamond. It's the diamond my mother handed down to me from my father, the jewel from her wedding ring that is now part of my own.

I was the victim of a common scam in Paris, I learned later from locals. One person distracts the woman while the other tries to remove her ring.

My hand felt violated and dirty. But mostly I felt like a chump. The thief had targeted me, I assume, because I was unaware.

Life is dangerous when we don't pay attention, whether we're walking through throngs of tourists or agreeing to get married when we aren't yet ready. That's a lesson my father's diamond should have taught me.

I can't wish my parents hadn't married on my mother's lunch hour. Otherwise, I wouldn't exist.

I also can't wish I didn't know the whole story. Pretending my parents' marriage was as idyllic as Paris in springtime would be lying about who I am.

This is what I tell myself about the diamond now. Its surface reminds me of the resiliency my father taught me. When he didn't buy me another balloon after mine popped, when he pulled me out of the safety of a playpen, when he let me fall off a bouncy horse then kiss my own boo-boos, he was training me for a world that didn't suffer fools or sissies. He knew how cruel people could be, calling him a freak, or rejecting him for jobs just because he lost his hand. If I wasn't going to get crushed, I would have to be hard. Like a diamond.

I won't let anyone yank it off. But if I decide to remove it, I can. A little soap is all it takes to slip it from my finger.

MY MOTHER AND I WERE alone again on Monday, hand-washing dishes together in a kitchen that could barely fit one. "Speaking of your dad . . ." Lately, she liked to begin conversations that way, as if we'd been in the middle all along. Then she'd pause, waiting for me to finish the sentence.

"I was thinking about when you two met," I said. "When did you find out about his hand?"

"I first met him when he came into the A&W root beer stand with Barry and I took their order. That was the fall of 1962. And that was when I first noticed his bandaged arm."

"How exactly did he lose his hand?"

She stacked the dishes in the drying rack. "How about some tea?" We boiled the water. Poured it into the cup. And steeped.

At the narrow table separating the dining area from the living room, I stirred milk so I wouldn't burn my tongue. I waited.

"I never knew how it happened," my mother finally said. "All these years, I never got the details."

I filled the space between us with questions. Suggestions. Was he working on a construction job? Demolition?

"He was just playing around." She swallowed.

"Playing with dynamite? What does that mean?"

We drained our tea.

"What did he tell you about the accident when you met?" I asked.

"He said the FBI pulled him and Barry in. Held them in there and interrogated them."

I didn't say, "You knew he had just been interrogated by the FBI, and you dated him *anyway?*" There's a scene from Martin Scorsese's *Goodfellas,* in which a young Mafia recruit meets his future wife for the first time. The gun in his jacket is a shock. She reels back, then changes her mind. "Some girls might have been turned off," she says in the voice-over. "But I was excited."

My mother said "FBI" so matter-of-factly. No explanation. No details.

"Why didn't you tell me before?"

"You never asked."

I still wasn't ready to think the worst, that my father was trying to blow something up to make a point, that his intent was anything but benign. But Noah was nineteen so I had an idea what kids that age were like. They're like kids. Could I imagine my son doing something impulsive and immature and dangerous, perhaps on a dare, something he could regret for the rest of his life? Absolutely.

NOW THAT I KNEW ABOUT the FBI, I imagined their meeting this way.

She walks to his car to pick up the orange tray hanging from his half-opened window. He pays then asks for her phone number, so she pulls out a pen from her apron and writes it on the back of his check. Where to look? Not at his hand, she doesn't mean to do that. But she's too shy to gaze straight into his face.

He lifts up his arm and shows her his bandage. He's not ashamed—why should he be? This injury is not going to define his life. He's already decided he will prove all the people wrong who say he can't do the work of a two-handed man. He'll do that and more. He'll be the best welder on any job. Buy a house and a car and pay it off just like that. He's got nothing to hide. If he's going to date this girl, she might as well know upfront who he is. He doesn't want to waste his time on girls who won't even look at him. Superficial girls. Girls who only care about appearances. This one, though, there's something kind about her. He can tell she has her own wounds, something about her soft voice and quiet moves. Her manner belies a seriousness most girls her age don't yet possess. A depth. He can trust her not to laugh. Even the way she takes his order is gentle.

"You're wondering what happened to me," he says. It's not a question, it's a statement.

"Yeah," he says, shooting a knowing glance at Barry. "So is the FBI."

Does she shudder, hearing he's on the wrong side of the law? She's already agreed to go out with him. Are any qualms superseded by the thrill of adventure? Maybe she is swept up in his confidence, entranced by his wavy red hair and green eyes, his slim but muscular build, his confidence and charisma.

"What did the FBI do?" I asked. "What did they find out? Was he arrested?"

"I don't know," my mother said.

She rose and started toward the bathroom. "I'm going to go clean up. Can't be as scuzzy in Paris as I am in Michigan."

I wanted to take a shower too. To start again, fresh.

"You want to know anything more about your dad," she said. "You have to ask Uncle Barry."

There was only one thing to do. It was time to go home.

Part 4
Season of Grief

Overleaf: My mother and Aunt Gail, 1990

August 2013

As soon as we touched down on American tarmac, Ella fell ill. If you asked her, she'd say she was homesick for Paris. Who knew *pain au chocolat* withdrawal could cause a fever? Just as I'd itched for Manhattan as a child, imagining it as the center of all beauty, she now yearned for her own big city.

Maybe she inherited my restless genes. My most vivid memories of growing up in Detroit involve hatching plans to get out of town. At fourteen, I'd started using my paltry paychecks to subscribe to *The Village Voice*, *The New Yorker*, and *The Poetry Project Newsletter* from St. Marks Church on the Lower East Side, then I applied only to colleges in New York City. Now Ella subscribed to *Mon quotidien*, the French daily newspaper for children, and told people "my soul is European."

Back in Virginia, as Ella clung to cotton scarves and strappy sandals, it didn't take me long to adjust to the downwardly mobile standards of American grooming. I grocery shopped with shower-wet hair and tucked my heels in a storage box next to Eiffel Tower ornaments.

Ella barely had time to recover from the flu before we boarded another plane, this time to California. My father-in-law was dying.

When Bob crashed his car a few months earlier, his bones and bruises healed. Now he was diagnosed with congestive heart failure. The heart just stops working.

We rented a car and drove from the Orange County Airport on vast seven-lane roads swarming with Ferraris, lined with palm trees and gleaming office buildings. Ronald Reagan territory.

A security guard beeped us into the gated community where James's parents lived, a childless 1970s development of cul-de-sacs, calla lilies, and signs warning us to "beware of coyotes" that were either local legend or invisible. James's mother Tricia answered the door. A trim woman in her seventies with close-cropped curly hair, she wore pressed khakis and a sweatshirt that read "So Many Books, So Little Time." And so little sleep, I could see from her sunken eyes.

The split-level architecture made mobility impairment especially challenging. The front door opened to a landing between two flights. Bob motored down in a mechanical seat attached to the railing. Once a serious hiker and jogger, he now couldn't even mount the stairs in his house. He was losing his sight, his height, and his hearing. He was disappearing. Bob leaned on a cane to stand, shrunken like a jack o' lantern left too long on the porch. "Who is it?" he asked Tricia, nodding toward James.

All the air seeped out of my husband's body. He hadn't seen his father in over a year, since we'd lived overseas. Were we too late?

The next day Bob recognized us. But we still strained to hold on to something escaping. A balloon leaking its helium. A heart losing its beat.

James took Ella to a repair shop to retrieve his parents' TV. Tricia was about to leave for a board meeting for the agency where she'd volunteered for the past quarter century, and Bob needed babysitting. "What do you want me to do?" I asked as she bustled out the door.

"Call 911 if anything happens." Don't let him die.

For the few hours of my solitary watch, I hovered at Bob's bedroom door, listened to his halting breath, stilled my own breathing and body noises enough to hear every one of his, over the threshold. I willed his heart to keep pumping.

If only that were enough.

The way children blame themselves when their parents divorce, part of me wondered if my father's death had been my fault. If I'd

loved him the way a daughter should, would he have valued his life
enough to be more careful with it?

I couldn't keep my own father safe. I couldn't stop him from
driving out into the dark fog. I couldn't make him wear a seatbelt.
Small children are so powerless. I didn't even say goodbye as he left
for his trip that night. I let him die. I wasn't about to do that again,
with my father-in-law.

When James returned with his parents' newly repaired TV, Bob
mustered his creaky strength enough to motor up the stairs in his
chair. We turned on the Angels game. For those few moments of
suspense, between the pitcher's throw and the crack of the bat, the
players acted as Bob's guardians. While the ball flew in the air, he
seemed to float above his illness too.

A WEEK LATER WE RETURNED to Virginia, and I called my mother
to arrange for her annual Halloween visit. I sat cross legged on my
bed while Ella read Asterix comics in French in her room across the
hall. My stepfather Joe answered the phone. "How's everything?" I
asked.

"Fine, fine," he said, as usual. Unlike my mother, he is an oiled
motor and words slide easily from his mouth. Though I almost
never know how he is really feeling, he always has something to say.
Almost always. This time he paused. Then handed the phone to my
mother.

I closed my bedroom door and climbed under the covers. Like
other rooms in our hundred-year-old house, this one is framed with
dark oak around the windows, and more on floors and doors.

"I was going to call you," my mother said, her voice rusty like a
hinge. She paused, much longer than Joe had. "It's Gail."

"What happened?" I already half-knew. "She died?"

I could almost hear my mother nod into the phone. I imagined
her sitting in her own bedroom, on a floral bedspread, gazing at a
display of family photos on the dresser, with frames that said things
like "too cute" and "World's Best Grandma."

I could hear her inaudibility. Her breath escaped in clipped, heavy puffs. I could hear her withholding for my benefit. I could hear her trying not to be heard. I could hear her *not* saying no. I could hear her break in half. My mother's twin died when she was six months old. Gail, eleven years younger, was her *real* twin, her spiritual other self. Her baby sister, whom she mothered her whole life. Gail was only fifty-six. Of seven children, now only two remained, my mother and Aunt Mary.

"How did she die?" Gail was a heavy smoker. Lung cancer would have been my guess.

"Breast cancer," my mother said.

"So quickly?"

"They found it in her eyes."

"In her *eyes?*"

"She went to the doctor because she was going blind. They did some tests. I guess the cancer got to her brain."

"But it started in her breasts?" I must have entered a weird Operation game, with the breasts connected to the eyes, wish bone connected to the funny bone. *Please tell me this is a joke.*

But my mother wasn't a joker. "That's their guess. It spread so much they didn't really know."

"She must have been in a lot of pain."

"Her doctor kept calling it arthritis."

"What?" What kind of quack would say that?

Gail was limited to doctors who treated patients with Medicaid. She'd been diagnosed with bipolar disorder early in life and lived off disability benefits. Gentle, kind, and unassuming, she was the type of person who would never ask for a second opinion, who didn't question doctors or other authority figures, who tried not to make a fuss. Someone like my mother. Or, in some ways, me.

I couldn't help imagining my mother neglecting her health and letting her doctor ignore her pain the way Gail had. If my mother had a fatal disease, I could picture not finding out till I called her house. Joe would answer and say, "Sorry I can't pass you on to her." Then he'd be forced to tell me it was too late to even attend her funeral.

Gail babysat my brother, sister, and me when my mother went on dates. In some small way, she was a surrogate parent. She was so young, her death so painful and graphic. I closed my eyes and could see a vicious army of cancer cells marching up from the breast to the brain to the eyes. The body host to invaders unknown, invisible, undetected. Her doctor told her she was a hypochondriac. "Don't be such a whiner," he might have said. Or maybe, "You welfare queens are always demanding special treatment." I needed to vent my spleen at someone, and I didn't know this doctor, so I chose him. I opened my eyes, but my vision turned cloudy, my breasts sore, my stomach woozy.

My mother didn't tell me anything when Gail was sick. I never had a chance to see her again. I didn't even get a call to invite me to the funeral. I have discovered every death of my mother's siblings this way, by calling her about something else. I heard Aunt Bonnie had died when I called to tell my mother I was pregnant with Ella. When I'd phoned to announce that James and I were engaged, my mother gave me her news before I could say a word, the news that Uncle Joe was gone. Every time, it was too late for me to publicly mourn with family.

"I kept meaning to call you." I believed that she *meant to.* "I wanted to call when James was home." So he could hold me while I cried? I wished he were here to hold me now, but even more, I wanted to be back in Detroit, resting my mother's head on my shoulder. "I'd plan to call. But every night I'd look at the clock. And every night it was too late," she told me on the phone. Yes, it was always too late.

"Can I come see you anyway?" I asked.

"It's not a good time," she said. "Nina is in hospice too." Aunt Nina, my mother's brother Anthony's wife. "Lung cancer." Anthony had died of bone marrow cancer not much more than a year before.

I didn't know what to say. I didn't know what I felt. Now I would call it shock. I was numb.

I wanted to stay on the phone long enough to be able to offer *something*. After one of our long silences, my mother asked, "What will Ella be for Halloween?"

Maybe a ghost. Like Gail and Anthony and Bonnie and Joe. Like Nina and Bob will soon be. Like God knows who's next.

At the time I wondered why my mother so quickly changed the subject. Her brusqueness struck me as cold. But later I realized she couldn't talk about Gail without breaking down. That evening, Aunt Mary told me in an e-mail that they couldn't even mention Gail's name without tears.

I spun around my house, almost tripping down the stairs. The story of my aunt's end disoriented me. Breast cancer doesn't blind people. Her death came too quickly after the diagnosis. Why hadn't she received preventive care? Why had her doctor dismissed her pain? And why did I have to mourn by myself in my kitchen? Rites are an essential part of every human society for a reason, our need to band together in our grief as primal as our need for sex and food. In Aunt Mary's e-mail, she said that Gail didn't even have a funeral I could have attended. When I read that I cried.

I didn't want my brother learning about Gail the way I did. Accidentally.

James was due home in half an hour, so I started dinner then dialed my brother. I paced the kitchen, stirring risotto and goading Ella to finish her math homework instead of reading recipes for mocktails in the *New York Times*. I asked Louis, "Are you mad?"

"Of course. Those shoddy Medicaid doctors should be put in jail."

"I mean at Mom."

"No." I imagined him, dressed in a vintage tweed suit with a bow tie and suspenders, in his university office, a fortress of beautiful objects and whimsical artifacts, surrounded by Italian Renaissance art history books. It has taken him decades to achieve the kind of calm I heard on the phone, and I envied it. He said, "She used to drive me crazy, she was so closed up. But now I understand. After what her mother did to her—calling us and saying our mother was a witch—Mom didn't have much left. She gave us all she had."

"This is not the way we should have heard about Gail," I said.

"Maybe not. But by now we should know."

I dribbled hot broth into the rice, scraping the bottom, as the steam opened my pores and almost burned me too. "Know what?"

"That if we want to find out about anything, we have to *ask*."

AT DINNER, OVER FRIED CHICKEN thighs and collard greens, James asked if I'd planned my trip to Michigan. I tried to explain that Uncle Barry might see me as a traitor as soon as he discovered I wanted to ask about the FBI. That I could lose him the way I lost my sister. As long as we stayed in Paris, I had an excuse not to call or visit.

"You always think people will be mad at you, but they never are," James said.

Unless you counted my sister. I always counted my sister.

Only Noah understood. While he was on break from college, we stayed up late, just the two of us, watching B movie Westerns and listening to comics' podcasts. We sprawled on the futon couch in the TV room, in jeans and T-shirts, dressed more identically than we had in Paris, where I'd tried to maintain a veneer of chic. Noah sipped Tension Tamer tea. "You know why I like stand-ups so much? They're just as scared shitless as me."

"So am I," I said.

"Yeah. What if everybody hates you when you start asking questions?"

"Exactly."

I sipped my Stella and handed him the bottle. Handcuff me right now for offering alcohol to my underage son. At nineteen, he'd been legal to drink in Paris.

Noah usually avoided even mentioning his own father to me. It's strange how these patterns repeat themselves over generations.

Maybe it was the beer talking then when he said, "I wish I knew more about my dad. His family too."

"What do you want to know?" I took another sip and listened. I told myself to answer honestly but without judgment. We talked for hours, deep into the night. My mother and I never did this when I was Noah's age. Because I never asked her to.

I'd imagined myself doing my mother a favor by being the low-maintenance daughter, the self-reliant middle child, the one she didn't have to worry about. I left home right after high school and prided myself on not asking for much. What I didn't acknowledge is that I didn't *offer* much either. By moving away so early and definitively, physically and emotionally, I'd stolen something valuable from her.

DAYS LATER, WHEN I DROVE Noah back to school, he slid the passenger-side seat of the Corolla so far he was almost in the rear. He was big and he liked to stretch his legs.

I usually dreaded driving, yet road trips with Noah were different. There's something about the cramped, enclosed space of a car that opens him up. When we drive together my son talks to me.

"Anxious about going to back to school?" Even though he no longer had the roommate from hell (who didn't launder or shower till Thanksgiving), he was still taking a long time to find friends.

I couldn't stop asking these kinds of direct questions, but that didn't mean he had to answer them. He just said, "You still scared about going back to Michigan?"

"Did I tell you the story about the FBI?"

"What?"

"I guess I didn't."

"That's why you're scared? The FBI is involved?" He leaned forward and craned his neck toward me.

"My mom told me in Paris that my dad and Uncle Barry were interrogated by the FBI after they set off some dynamite."

"What did the FBI charge them with?"

"I don't know."

"What did Granny say?"

"She said, Ask Uncle Barry."

"But he's not going to tell you. If nobody's told you yet, there's a reason it's a secret." Blood filled his cheeks, his voice charged with adrenaline. My family had a *story.* Something screen worthy, maybe. Noah tried to see every major film on the day it was released. The car sped over seventy, and I floored the gas to pass a posse of trucks.

"Don't go," Noah said.

"I have to get around these nimrods. Look at them swerving. They're probably eating doughnuts and texting."

"Don't go to Michigan." He squirmed, squeaking his feet on the floor pad. "Why make people uncomfortable?"

"I want to know."

"But you also don't want to know."

"You think that's weird?" I asked.

"No," he said. "I'm like that all the time."

After two hours of driving, we pulled into the parking lot of Food Lion so Noah could stock his dorm kitchen. He cradled a dozen eggs and a half gallon of milk, not bothering to pick up a basket. A carton of coffee filters. A box of pasta and a jar of sauce. "Here, let me help," I said. I was always trying to help him. He was over eighteen, technically an adult, but my reflex was to butt in. It was a physical, automatic response, like ducking to dodge a ball. Did I grab the jar, abruptly catching him off guard, or am I just clumsy? Did he struggle with me, insisting on juggling his burdens himself? Whatever the cause, I dropped the marinara smack in the middle of the aisle and it splattered like blood. I couldn't have made more of a mess if I'd been prepping for a B movie gore scene.

"Shit." I grabbed another jar from the shelf.

Noah fled as if he'd heard a gunshot. I found an employee and pointed out the spill. A voice over the loudspeaker summoned a mop-up crew for aisle six.

After I paid, I walked out to the car, where he was waiting for me.

"Did they charge for the broken jar?" he asked, after I unlocked the door.

"No. It was an accident."

"But haven't you seen the signs in stores? You break it, you buy it."

"We're not talking antique porcelain here." I started the ignition.

"If *I* had broken the jar, I would have left the store without my groceries," he said.

"Really?"

"I probably would have found a different place to shop next time."

I hit the gas pedal and reversed. "Everybody makes stupid mistakes. That's no reason to run away."

AFTER DROPPING NOAH OFF, I started the two-hour drive home alone, the empty road stretching with memories of stupid mistakes I'd made, of things left unsaid. When I was Noah's age, I didn't ask about the past. I didn't try to coax out my mother's stories. Instead, I made up my own.

I'd been running away my whole life, without stopping to pick up the pieces of myself I'd left behind, convinced, without evidence, that people who liked me now would not accept me if they knew who I'd been. A tragic children's book character. An orphan.

Noah, at least, could voice his impulse to cut and run. I wanted to become as honest as my teenage son. I wanted to see, again, what he was trying to show me.

I merged onto the highway. I wasn't used to long drives by myself, especially not in the dark. An hour into the trek back to Charlottesville, dusk settled in a smoky blue haze. The clouds smeared like watercolor.

I played a CD Noah gave me for Christmas, from the hip-hop group Atmosphere. "When Life Gives You Lemons, You Paint That Shit Gold." I play it all the time. I play it in the car. In the gym. On my walks. On my runs. Waiting at the bus stop for Ella. Washing dishes or cleaning the toilet.

"Yesterday," my favorite, came on. At first it seems like a break-up song, an elegy to a long-lost love.

> I'm sorry, it's official
> I was a fist-full, I didn't keep it simple
> Chip on the shoulder, anger in my veins
> Had so much hatred, now it brings me shame
> Never thought about the world without you
> And I promise that I'll never say another bad word about you

The twist at the end surprises me every time.

> I thought I saw you yesterday
> But I knew it wasn't you, 'cause you passed away . . .
> Dad

"I'm sorry," I said. The six empty seats in my Odyssey didn't respond. Neither did my father.

The road unraveled. The sky dimmed to muted, crepuscular grays, that time between night and day, that crack between two worlds.

In the fall deer get hungry, which makes them reckless. They dart across the road when your guard is down.

That's why I never wanted to drive. I felt like the sole Motor City teen who didn't apply every one of my fast-food paychecks toward a car. I didn't want to share the road with deer. Yet look, I moved out here, to their domain.

A flash of fur filled my windshield. No antlers. A doe and a fawn maybe. One, a blurry line in my long-distance periphery; then the other, a swatch of light-colored fur in my brights.

The vast hollow innards of my minivan echoed with my heartbeat. Way over the speed limit.

THAT FALL, THE LONGER I postponed talking to my uncle, the more I forgot my coat, my keys, my lunch. I locked myself out and I couldn't sleep.

I was going to interrogate him like the police. Like the FBI. Like the enemy. I knew my father's family hated the cops, though I never knew why. Maybe I would to find out.

I would travel to the woods of northern Michigan where I spent many wild summer days as a child, first with my family and then, after my father's death, with my grandparents. We used to drive four hours from the city starting at four in the morning. We would arrive at eight, the whole day ahead of us.

This trip would be my first return since I moved from Michigan for college and for good. I'd returned to Detroit ("Downstate," as we Michiganders call it), the place I was raised, many times. But northern Michigan, where my grandparents and ancestors were born, is my spiritual home. The pipelines overgrown with blackberry brambles, the red pines, the white pines, the salt licks for game, the deer blinds. The place my people come from. The place so much of *me* came from, though that piece remained beyond reach for so long.

One day in October, I sat at my desk, the door closed behind me, and finally managed to e-mail my uncle. I said I wanted to ask him about my father, then I listed a few questions. When I hit Send I knew there was no turning back.

Barry called me immediately. His voice sounded so close to what I either remembered or imagined of my father's cadences that I startled as if a ghost were on the other line. "I'm surprised you don't know the answers to those questions," he said.

I exhaled and paused. I'm not good on the phone. My voice shrinks, like a child's. I melt into a breathy whisper. I finally said, "So am I."

I was even less prepared to hear the next thing he said, "Your sister asked me those same questions. Twenty years ago."

Two whole decades I'd been ignorant of things my sister knew. She never told me. I never asked.

"We can talk about all this in person," Barry said. "You're coming to visit, right?"

"Yes." I guess I was. I hung up and booked my flight.

JAMES'S SISTER LIZ CALLED IN the middle of dinner a few days later. "You might have to cancel your trip to Michigan," James said after hanging up.

"Your dad?"

"No, my mom. She's in the emergency room. A neighbor called an ambulance after she collapsed on the driveway."

Tricia didn't have a heart attack. She didn't have a stroke. She fainted from exhaustion, a casualty of caretaking. James bought a plane ticket so he could help nurse his father and arrange for hospice. The night before his flight we sat on our covered porch, sipping bourbon on ice and listening to the residual fall buzz of cicadas, the soft African drumming of our neighbor on his porch, the fuzzy drift from an outdoor concert half a mile away. "My dad's dying," James said.

"I know." It was all we talked about that fall. Fathers and death. The doctor predicted Bob would last one to six months.

"At least he had a good life," I said. "At least he lived a long time. At least you got to say good bye." At least, at least, at least. I didn't say that Bob was eighty-seven, fifty-five years older than my father had been. I didn't have to say it; James knew what I meant. "It could have been worse."

"That's not helpful."

I swirled my bourbon and rocked. I filled his glass and squeezed his shoulders, trying to melt the tension the way the alcohol burned through the ice. He bristled.

"What would be helpful?"

"Nothing." He put his hand over my lips. "Just this." This silence. This attentive, tender listening. To the scuffle of skunks and groundhogs under the porch. To the sleeping sparrow nested into the corner, above a wooden pillar. To the wind chilling us so much we had to lean in closer to each other's body heat. To the cats pouncing and stalking. To the porch light buzzing and the bugs sizzling their tails on its shock.

The next morning, after Ella boarded the school bus, I helped James pack. He stood in his underwear fresh from the shower when I handed him the phone. His sister called to say the doctor changed Bob's prognosis. He now had only two to seven days.

"My father's going to die while I'm *there*," James wailed after hanging up. He stood in his bleached white briefs, his pink skin bare and goosepimply from the chill and the bad news, looking as vulnerable as a baby in nothing but a diaper. He started to babble, to walk around semi-naked and repeat himself. He couldn't fold a shirt or find a tube of toothpaste. I'd never seen him like this. He can be moody. He can be angry. But incompetent? Never.

I fished out a tube of Sensodyne and stacked a neat pile of white undershirts on the bed, but mostly I listened. All his adult veneer had slipped away. He was a kid again, pining for his daddy. He mumbled and repeated and stumbled. "It's going to happen while I'm there." He sat on the edge of the bed and rocked. "I can't do it." James never says that. But this is what grief does—it removes a part of us. The part that forgets every day that everyone we love is going to die. That we are too.

I didn't try to calm him. Grief is not like the measles. It's not something we can inoculate ourselves against. We have to allow the loss to run its course, the pox to blister and ooze.

James had to teach two classes before he boarded his flight, and he asked me to go to work with him, something he had never done before. "I can't teach without crying," he said.

"Tell your students about your dad. So they'll know why you're choking up."

James was a man of his time. Perhaps the first generation of men who could cry.

Some of his students sent him e-mails after class, expressing their sympathy and telling their own stories of loss.

"I wish you could come to California," James told me, but I had to stay with Ella. He hyperventilated in the car as we drove to the airport. He never did that. "I'm so scared," he said. He was never scared. Maybe this is what happens to people when their fathers die. They become unrecognizable. "I've never been like this," he said, "except maybe when Ella was about to be born."

We know so little about where we come from, where we go. Arrivals and departures in some ways feel the same.

AFTER TWO DAYS THE PHONE call arrived. The call I knew would come. "He's gone." James told me he and Tricia had held Bob's hand in his bed at home and heard him take his last breath then settle into quiet. "It was beautiful. Such a peaceful send-off." James sent me a picture of Bob's breathless body. He looked asleep. His usually clean shaven face was covered in a scruffy goatee that transformed him, incongruously, into a Brooklyn hipster.

James's voice was slow and steady. Weirdly calm. "It was a privilege to be with him at the end," he said. "I'm sure my siblings wish they'd been here too."

The deathbed photo didn't have the same effect on me. I couldn't look at it without shivering. "You were so scared," I said.

"I'm not anymore. You wouldn't be, either. It was so peaceful, the way he drifted off. I'll try to remember that when my time comes."

I wondered what kind of magic James must have experienced. I wanted to lean in close to death too, if that would bring me such supernatural steadiness. I wasn't able to hold my own father's hand when he died, but I could try to imagine what it would have been like.

I hung up and entered Ella's bedroom, where she was reading time travel books. When I told her Grandpapa died, she chanted, "Why? Why? Why?" My normally happy-go-lucky daughter crossed over to the other side, the side that understands that death is real.

I didn't tell her not to cry. I didn't say, "At least Grandpapa lived a long life." I let her wail. And I listened.

I will miss my father-in-law. I am grateful that he welcomed me into the family with warmth and enthusiasm. But my husband and daughter's grief was more primal, the kind that turns your life into Before and After. You never forget your first. I've never forgotten mine. Losing my father was the most significant thing that happened to me. My daughter will always remember when she learned—on a personal and visceral level—that all beginnings come to an end.

She pulled a dictionary off the shelf and read aloud the definition for death. Then she flipped further and read the definition of love. Don't we all wish we could find the answers to life's mysteries in reference books? Maybe she was trying to tell me that love is the one thing that doesn't die.

What do we say to help absorb the grief of others? In the days and weeks after, when Ella cried in the middle of a store or a story or a playdate, I handed her a tissue.

"Why did Grandpapa have to die?"

I smoothed her unruly hair and kissed the top of her head.

"I loved him," she said. "He loved me."

"I know."

"Why do people we love have do die? Why? Why?"

I'd been asking myself that question since I was seven.

MY MOTHER WAS SCHEDULED TO arrive the next day. "Should I cancel her visit?" I asked James.

"No," he said, on the phone. "But she may have to leave early."

The funeral wasn't yet scheduled. Bob would be cremated, which meant his service could be days or weeks later.

"Should I cancel my trip to Michigan?" My flight to interrogate my uncle was in ten days.

"Not yet," he said.

It would have been convenient to have an excuse to bail. To put off a trip that filled me with foreboding, though I still didn't know why.

On Halloween, I picked up my mother from the airport. I had sent a note to school alerting Ella's teachers that her grandfather died. I told them that if she started to cry in class, they could call me and I'd take her home.

Normally Ella rode the bus and walked the block home by herself. When my mother and I pulled into our driveway, my phone rang. It was Ella. She'd been waiting in the school office. Her teachers misunderstood my note and told her not to take the bus.

Ella's school is not far. But I made a wrong turn and lost my way. I was so disoriented I had to pull the GPS out of my glove compartment and punch in the school's address.

"What took you so long?" Ella asked, when I arrived.

"I don't know." I couldn't tell her my internal compass was broken.

In the evening, I forgot the gorgon head from Ella's Halloween costume three times and had to return home for it. My competence was leaching away. That's what I'd seen with James the day of his flight. Was I grieving directly for Bob? Sharing my husband's grief? Reliving my father's death, set on a continuous loop because I'd never grieved fully or maturely for him? Yes.

I slipped on a mask. A bat head. Then bat wings. If every night were Halloween, no one would ever have to see us cry.

Ella and two of her friends trick-or-treated together as the three Gorgons, Medusa and her sisters, so dangerous that one glance at them could turn a mortal into stone. All the local children gathered for the annual costume parade. It's a festive time, one I look forward to every year, reuniting with neighbors and parents of Ella's friends. "Where's James?" they all inevitably asked, and I had to say, "His father died yesterday."

"Hold hands!" all the mothers seemed to shout in unison. The fathers roared, "Stay out of the street!" "Car!" one of them said, which elicited a choral response, "Watch out!"

Just days before, on the street where the parade started, a six-year-old girl was killed by a truck. We weren't frightened by vampires or zombies. Cars were the big bad wolf, the bear in the forest, the predator on the prowl.

Once I returned home and put Ella to bed, I told my mother about the recent fatal accident. I didn't have to explain that I can't think of car crashes without remembering the one in our family.

I slipped off my wings, stuffed my feet into slippers, and poured myself a glass of Cotes du Rhone.

My mother opened a mini Twix. "Remember when your sister was hit by a car?" she asked.

"She was?"

"You don't remember?"

I coaxed the story out of my mother, bit by bit. Lynn was fourteen, walking to school in the morning. A woman was driving with her windshield frosted over, hadn't even bothered to scrape it off. Lynn was dragged underneath while crossing the street. She had to go to the hospital.

I willed myself to bring that episode back to the surface. Did my forgetfulness mean I didn't care? How could that be?

I bit down on my thumb. "What *I* remember is Louis getting hit by a car. He was little. We were in the playground at Keppen School and he rode his bike into the street. An ambulance came, and you climbed in with him. Kimmy's family took me home."

"I wouldn't have sent you home with Kimmy's family," she said. "They were bullies."

"You don't remember?" I asked.

Strange how people in my family have different pieces of memories. How many would we have to collect to assemble an entire story? Our lives are so fragmented. Like pasta sauce jars breaking and scattering shards all over the grocery store floor.

Out the dining room window, a car skidded. A cat squealed. *Just stay out of the street. Everyone. Go home.*

THE DAY AFTER HALLOWEEN, MY mother and I sat on the bleachers next to the pool, as Ella backstroked and butterflied past us, part of her weekly lesson with Miles, her hunky teenage coach. Ella mostly disappeared underwater, but Miles was far from invisible, strutting the length of the pool and shouting instructions to her in nothing but a minuscule Speedo and black hipster glasses. The sylphs gliding through the other lanes made me feel like Jell-O stuffed in mom jeans.

We breathed chlorine and bathed in warmth, drifting from the heated pool, its spiral slides and sprinklers newly added. Ella whizzed by in the cold pool's lap lanes, under dolphin sea glass mosaics. Sun streamed through skylights.

My phone beeped. I read a text from James in California, asking my advice on preparations for his father's funeral. He wanted me to help edit the bios for the program and the newspaper.

I knew it was antisocial to text when I should have kept my mother company, but I thought it would be less rude if I shared with her the gist of our conversation. She listened and nodded, then asked, "You remember your dad's funeral?" Everything, this season, led back to him.

"A little," I said. "I remember big crowds."

She told me so many people came, not just because he died young, but because he was so respected as a welder. He gave himself no slack for his missing hand. He more than compensated. "With his ingenuity, he could do anything."

Not everyone thought so, though. "He had to get thick skinned," my mother said, "to deal with the obstacles thrown his way."

"Like what?"

"He applied to work at Ford and after they sent him for a physical they told him he was disqualified because of a hernia. He did not have a hernia. They rejected him because of his hand."

Maybe all those rejections were part of what made him grow hard. I wondered what they would have done to me. I clenched my fist and pounded my knee, wanting to fight. For the vulnerable among us, victims of discrimination. For my father.

"They had to use three rooms instead of one," she said. "I've never been to another funeral with so many people."

"How many?"

"I don't know. I could tell you if I had the guest book."

"What happened to it?"

"Grandma took it."

"Wasn't it yours?" She was next of kin.

"She wanted it so much."

"Who has it now?" I needed to see it, to count the names and finger the ink of the signatures. So few objects remain, so little physical proof.

"I looked for it in Grandma's house. After she died," my mother said. "She must have tossed it. Accidentally, of course. After the stroke."

"Do you still have the dress you wore?"

"No. I have a picture, though."

"Of the funeral?"

"The dress." She pulled an album from her copious purse. "I brought these to make copies for you. You told me you don't have many photos."

I didn't realize she'd been listening.

My mother leafed through her album and pointed to a picture of herself in a turquoise jersey turtleneck dress. "This was taken a little after he died. It's the same one I wore to the funeral."

"You wore a blue dress?" I was sure she wore black. I thought I remembered it so clearly. In the story I always told myself about the funeral, she's costumed in a stiff black frock. Much more formal than this one. I was going to wear a stiff black dress to my father-in-law's funeral. Isn't that what everyone did? Was I substituting a scene from a movie for one in real life?

I turned off my phone and intertwined my hands.

She looked both ways to make sure we were alone. "I bought that dress the day after your dad died. Grandma took me shopping at Sears." Grandma, my father's mother, was the most practical person I've ever met, the one who could be counted on in any situation to get things done. God knows she probably wanted to just stay in bed.

"But why couldn't you wear a dress you had? If it didn't need to be black?"

"I didn't have a dress that fit. Everything except maternity clothes were too small."

I'd seen plenty of pictures of my mother back then. She was slim. "You weren't pregnant?"

"No. But your dad thought I was too fat. He wouldn't let me buy clothes. Not till I could fit in the ones I wore at our wedding."

I waited. Pulled my bra straps back up over my shoulders. Wiped the sweat from my upper lip.

She said, "I was 120 pounds when we got married and 135 when he died."

"I was 120 pounds when I married James. I'm 135 now." My mother is five foot two, I'm five foot six, but still, the parallel is uncanny.

"You look great at that weight," my mother said.

I almost said, "I'm trying to lose ten pounds." But I stopped. I wanted to believe I looked beautiful, as lovely as my mother looked in the picture on my lap, her turquoise dress clinging to her sexy curves.

What would my father say about my own weight now? I need to believe he wouldn't criticize my mother or me. He'd even cheer on Ella's healthy appetite. He'd learn about the dangers of eating disorders, as I have, and be careful not to cause her to obsess about her body.

"I tried and tried and tried," my mother said. "I couldn't lose weight."

Ella pulled her eighty-pound body out of the pool and walked toward our bleachers. The lesson was over.

I didn't want Ella to hear the rest of the story. "Why don't you go play on the slide?" I said.

"I'm tired."

"Then go float on the lazy river. You worked hard."

"Look at my muscles." She flexed her puny biceps. Then she turned around and joined a group of other children.

"She's so strong," my mother said.

"Yeah." In my next life, I want to be reincarnated as my daughter.

"So I was saying . . ." my mother started. She hunched so close she almost whispered in my ear, her arms and legs tightened in attention. Our bodies warmed each other, the distance between us evaporating like the steam over the lazy river.

"A few days after your dad died, I lost all the weight without even trying. I didn't know why. Much later, my doctor explained. My birth control pills. They make you retain water. Once I stopped taking them, I lost fifteen pounds. Just like that. The hormones were so strong back then. All that weight was water."

We were trapped in some kind of morbid O. Henry story, where characters only get what they want when they can no longer use it. My mother became perfect for my father only after he was gone.

Ella splashed and waved at us. Water, water everywhere.

ON THE WAY BACK FROM the pool, we stopped at CVS so my mother and I could copy the photos of her funeral dress and a couple dozen others—of my lost aunts and uncles, many of Gail, some of Joe and Bonnie and Anthony too. And other photos I'd never seen of my mother's grandmother. Ella collapsed on the bed, too tired from all that swimming to do anything but watch YouTube videos on cake decorating. I let her take my iPad upstairs so my mother and I could look at more pictures at the dining room table.

"That's your great-grandmother Belle," my mother said. "You know I wanted to name you after her."

"Didn't Dad want to name me Nimrod?"

"If you were a boy. He said it was a great hunter from the Old Testament."

I like to think it didn't mean what it does now.

"Why didn't you name me Belle?"

"Your dad said it was a hillbilly name."

My mother's family came from Appalachia. As a child, I took the Greyhound bus and arrived in Barbourville, Kentucky, at four in the morning, just as the cocks began to crow. We ate delicious green beans slathered in bacon drippings and chicken and dumplings.

We walked barefoot on green hills, woke at the sound of roosters, scouted for snakes, and bought elegant glass bottles of ice-cold Coke from the general store. Belle is a common first and middle name down there. As a child, I imagined the Liberty Bell. Or a southern belle, the shape of her dress fanning out like an open umbrella. I didn't know then that Belle meant beautiful. I didn't know it was French and might have predicted my future.

"Know what's funny?" my mother said. "The doctor handed me the birth certificate. Your dad wasn't even in the room. The doctor said, 'Fill in the blank.' I could have written anything. I knew your dad wanted to name you Sharon so that's what I wrote."

It didn't occur to her then that she had a choice. About anything.

I know what she means. I'd thought the same thing too, at times, when I was young. It takes more than one generation to erase a society's history of teaching girls to be demure.

"You still think about it?"

"It's not like I argued. Another kind of woman would have fought for what she wanted."

I began to wonder whether my father even *knew* what my mother wanted. She was often tongue tied. She stuttered and stammered, especially when she was younger.

"I always think of you as Belle," my mother said. She stared at me intently, her jaw clenched, her gaze serious, as if a different name might have transformed me into a different kind of person.

"It's better than Nimrod," I said.

Her lips softened, her shoulders relaxed. She laughed at that.

I LEFT FOR MICHIGAN A day after Bob's funeral in California, in almost back-to-back flights, home long enough just to pack and leave.

Home? So much had happened since I'd returned from Paris, I was beginning to wonder what that word meant. As we zoomed through the clouds, I felt a pull, like the one that had yanked me toward Manhattan as a teen. I could now sense my body gravitating toward my ancestral home, the snowy woods of northern Michigan.

Alone for the first time in many days, I ate the airline-issued cookie and replayed my California trip, which had turned into a Harrigan family reunion.

All members of the nuclear family (except for the ones who lived within driving distance), plus James's aunts and uncles and cousins rented motel rooms along the same hallway. Ella's cousins played cards and swam in the motel pool, while James and his siblings and their spouses stayed up past midnight, unspooling yarns about a man who lived a long, upstanding life. A man who worked as a civil engineer, then retired and reinvented himself as a financial planner. A family man, with four children, ten grandchildren, and a devoted wife who cared for him for more than half a century. A hospice patient who died quietly in his bed.

During the wake all of us family members had gathered around a large table and took turns telling a story about Bob. All the adults seated, Tricia spontaneously asked everyone to offer an anecdote about their father or father-in-law. One of my husband's brothers, was the first to be called upon. Put on the spot, he hesitated, searching, sifting through a lifetime of memories for *the* memory; at last he excused himself, saying he didn't know what story to tell. His silence hung thick, like Southern California smog. The rest of the grown-ups took a turn. And then, after all the others had finished, the first brother was finally ready to share his own chosen memory, then so did the grandchildren.

We three generations pieced together a man who was reliable, trustworthy, and funny. An outdoorsman, man of God, and Civil War buff. But also, in some ways, an unknown. Bob traveled for months at a time, working overseas. He was the kind of man his generation was socialized to be, driven to earn enough to give his children an easier life than he'd had. He was a man of his time too.

Bob traveled so much, it was hard for his sons and daughter to remember spending much private time with him. This is the story of fathers of that generation.

The story of absence. Maybe Noah was thinking about that too as we walked through the Orange County Airport, on the way back from the funeral. His phone rang as we inched past security, and this time, at last, he answered it. "Hi Dad."

Maybe Noah was thinking that the story of absence doesn't have to be the end of the story. He could have been musing that he didn't want to find himself at his father's wake, not knowing what to say when it was his turn for an anecdote. Perhaps he was starting to realize that we could change the stories we tell.

I remember my father being largely absent too, even when he was alive. He worked such long hours, driven to prove his mother-in-law wrong when she predicted his disability would stop him from supporting a family. Maybe if he had lived to old age I still might not have ever known him well. Perhaps we all grieve in some way over the time we didn't spend with our fathers. Even people who aren't orphaned early might mourn their lost opportunities for intimacy. I took that realization home from California, like a parting gift, a gift I was remembering on this plane ride to Michigan, as I realized I was not as singular as I'd always thought.

I still wished my father had lived long enough for his children to grow up into adults who could regale each other with stories about him around the table, as we'd done for Bob. I wondered what people said at my father's funeral and what they would say now. The symmetry of my two November trips was striking. After traveling to my father-in-law's funeral, I felt almost as if I were continuing on to my father's.

Part 5

Downstate

Overleaf: My father and his best friend David, holding their sons, 1965

November 2013

I LANDED AT DETROIT METRO Airport. Absent my children, husband, and car, I shrank to child size.

This was Big Three country. Motor City. I pulled my carry-on from overhead and dragged it behind. Didn't I always take my baggage with me?

Through revolving doors, into pelting rain, I scanned ahead, looking for a pickup—Ford, GM, or Chevy. My uncle agreed to meet me outside Arrivals.

"Ask Barry," my mother had said in Paris. He knew the details she didn't. I wasn't sure I was ready to hear them, but I hadn't come all this way to chicken out now.

Where was he? I tramped the sidewalk, squinting through downpour. Even the clothes in my carry-on would smell like wet fur the whole week.

Then I saw him. Uncle Barry, in his familiar flannel shirt and blue jeans, stepped out of the driver's seat and shouted my name. Aunt Cora emerged from the passenger side, and they both hugged me before I dripped my way into the back. They looked so perpetually youthful and slim, I thought I hadn't stepped off a plane but a time machine. Barry had most of his hair, more than my much younger husband, and his beard leaned toward gray but still glimmered with red. My aunt's brown bob was cut in the half-tomboy/half Audrey Hepburn style I remember her wearing back when I was experimenting with cheesy feathered affairs in the eighties.

Barry started driving toward the airport exit. "You walked right past my car!"

"I didn't expect a Toyota," I said.

"What people don't understand," he said, "is that these cars have more American parts and are made with more American labor than your Ford or your Chevy. You need to do your research and then you see what's the most patriotic car in reality."

You need to do your research. I'd better get started.

MY UNCLE MERGED ONTO I-94 West to Carleton. Barry and Cora now lived much farther from the city than they did when I was young.

After we left the highway, the roads turned to dirt, the mailboxes spread out, and the houses receded behind long driveways. We passed the town of Flat Rock, where my father is buried, the place my grandparents visited almost every Sunday, often with us kids, to refresh the flowers on the grave. My mother took us too, partly an excuse to drive through this picturesque part of Michigan, scarcely a half hour from the city but a world away, full of farm stands and snowmobiles, the crunch of pebbles on the open road, the spacious smell of unpolluted sky.

Barry's car skirted around the city itself, the metropolitan area now like a doughnut with Detroit the hole in the middle. "It's snowing Up North," he said. "Not sure how soon we can go there. Might want to wait till the roads get cleared up."

"Fine with me." I'd put off revisiting my father's sacred place my whole adult life. Part of me hoped the ice would never melt.

We pulled into Barry and Cora's driveway then walked into their sprawling new house, giant compared to the one I grew up in. Though it occupies only one floor, it was designed with high ceilings and generously proportioned rooms that make it feel ample and airy. Cora played tour guide, showing me where the towels or toilet paper were, every corner of every closet organized in a way I envied but could never achieve. I wheeled my suitcase into my room, next to the bed dressed in a handmade quilt and lace-trimmed pillow-

cases. Then I melted into the couch next to the fireplace and prepared to do my research.

"You said you had some questions about your dad," my
uncle said. I loved the rhythms of Barry's midwestern speech,
the warm and welcoming lilt I lost after living so long out East.
My uncle's words slid into each other, their consonants as soft
as the couch, their vowels milky. There is so much play in the
way Uncle Barry talks; I can't convey the affectionate teasing, the
gentle familiarity, the chuckle and wink implied in his cadences.
I like to imagine my father's voice was as beckoning as this, but
I don't think it was. In my memory, Barry is the one who understood fun.

I excavated my phone from my front jeans pocket. "Mind if
I record?" I'd spent most of the plane ride worrying about all the
possible responses to that question. As Noah had said, these stories
had been secret so long *for a reason.*

"Go right ahead," my uncle said, as if I asked to use the bathroom.

I turned the tape recorder on.

BARRY STRETCHED HIS LEGS ACROSS the ottoman. "You said you
wanted to hear about the dynamite."

Bang. It couldn't be that easy. What had I expected—that he
would call my bluff and run me out of town for daring to unbury
something that should have stayed underground? He was nothing
but friendly and calm. I was the one knifing my nails into the tender skin of my fingers.

I wasn't prepared for the big questions yet—I thought we'd
build up to them with small talk, start off with light anecdotes like
people often do when I interview them for magazines. But then I
realized what should have been obvious. Just because it was hard
for me to hear what happened to my father didn't mean it was hard
for Barry to tell. So many years had passed. And he, unlike me, had
allowed himself to grieve.

"Yeah," I said. I might have just nodded. I couldn't believe that was all I had to do to start Barry's story machine. So why had I waited so long?

"We were blowing up them suckers," he began.

"Suckers?" I asked.

"Tree stumps," Cora said. "They were clearing the property Up North."

He huddled, his sixty-nine-year-old body still hale enough to take up all the stage presence in the room. "Okay. We had an old car we left running to recharge the battery. I was the one that fused the dynamite. The wind was blowing. And this is the spooky part."

I stared at the fire so long I could almost see a face in it. Maybe my father's. Maybe my own.

Barry plucked a bag of M&Ms and ripped it open. "We were standing there shielding the wind to get this fuse to light. And I got this funny feeling."

I could feel it too. A familiar twinge. The porcelain pilgrims and turkeys lining the shelves kept smiling at us anyway.

His voice lowered. "You could call it a premonition or something magic or religious. A ghost or God or a voice in my head. You could just call it knowledge of what *could* happen. I made this statement: 'If this damn thing goes off prematurely it's going to get all three of us.' Jerry said, *real calm,* 'That's right.' Then he held it tighter in his hand. We got it lit and me and Dave turned our backs to it. We each took one step away, and it went off."

Bang. I could almost hear it in the crackle from the hearth.

"I turned around, and of course it blew Jerry's whole hand. All he had was his thumb hanging by his tendon like this." Barry held up his arm so I could imagine flesh falling off the bone, chicken stewed too long on the stove.

"But if you and Dave hadn't taken that step back . . .," I started.

"It would have got us in the face and everything."

"They would have all got killed," Cora said.

Barry said, "Lucky we turned around. Lucky the car was sitting there running."

Lucky is the word he kept repeating to describe this horrific incident. If they'd had one drop less luck, my father would have died that day and I'd never have been born. Neither Barry nor I would be in this room chewing the fat and sucking a Kit Kat and drinking the coffee I hoped would quicken my heartbeat and brainwaves enough to shock-absorb this story.

"It's the same thing as slicing your wrist off," Barry said. What was the same? This lucky thing. "Because this was all gone." Barry karate-chopped the middle of his right forearm. "He was just squirting. I jerked them battery cables off, slammed the hood, threw Jerry in the front seat, Dave jumped in and made a makeshift tourniquet, and we went just as fast as we could go to Kalkaska." Where there was a small hospital.

I could see Dave as a junior medical emergency technician, maybe even a teenage medicine man. Dave must have *saved my father*. Maybe Barry could read my mind because he corrected me. "Dave was one of those people, under a stress situation, he blanks."

The tourniquet didn't work. Dave had no idea what he was doing. My uncle was too modest to voice the truth: *Barry* saved his brother's life. Dave wouldn't have been able to pull the cables out of the car so fast and floor the gas like hellfire to the hospital, which is what my uncle did.

Barry saved my father. I should have thanked him. I should have stopped his story long enough to grab him by the shoulders in a big hug. Big enough to contain my whole life.

But all I wanted at that moment was to hear what happened next. All I could say was, "What did my dad do?"

"Jerry just sat there, real calm, and said, 'I believe I lost my hand.' And I said, 'Yeah, you did.'"

I believe I lost my hand. With an arsenal of curse words at his disposal and a legendary temper, that's all he could muster? The sound of those words is so matter of fact and polite, so detached, so damn *calm*. You'd think he was uttering a perfectly banal statement: *I believe you have dialed the wrong number.*

"Wasn't he in a lot of pain?" I asked.

"Of course, but he was *extremely* calm."

Cora said, "He was in shock." Of course. Just as I was when my father died, which is why I couldn't cry. Shock is a natural anesthetic.

Barry said, "I was driving and I run cars off the road and everything else. When we got to the hospital they were standing there waiting for us."

"Waiting for you?"

"Jerry had bled the front wheel well full, the back wheel well full, and it was running out between the door and the rocker panel. I passed a car on the way, and I sprayed them with blood. And someone went in their house and called the hospital and told them we were on our way. Then Jerry transferred to Munson, which is where they actually did the surgery."

"In Traverse City," Cora said. The nearest decent-sized town.

"That's pretty far," I said.

"Yeah, but they got the bleeding stopped first, started putting IVs in him, got him kind of stabilized. He'd about bled out."

"What do you mean?"

"He'd about died. He probably didn't have another three minutes left in him."

Three minutes. The length of a long red light. The cooking time for a soft-boiled egg. If they'd gone 100 miles an hour instead of 120, they would have wasted much more than three minutes. If they'd lost their way or their nerve. If they'd sneezed or blinked, panicked or had to pee. Three minutes is nothing. I waste more than that every hour.

"My God." What could I say except a little prayer? Thank you for sparing my father's life long enough for me to be born. My Father in heaven, my father on earth, my father under the earth. My God.

Barry said, "You can imagine, on that '55 Ford, the wheel well's full, the back one's full, and it's running out over the rocker panels." A tub of blood. A blood bath.

YES, I COULD IMAGINE THE whole scene.

My father holds the dynamite stick, and Barry and Dave step away after Barry hears a warning, from God or his gut, that something bad is about to happen. He warns my father too, but instead of moving my father grips the stick more tightly, maybe because he's too analytical to believe in messages from God, maybe because it all happens too fast. Barry and Dave turn their backs and shuffle out of the way to safety.

Boom. My father's hand is blasted off.

And why? Because they were clearing the land, cleaning up the remains of old trees so new ones could be planted in their place. Taking care of the forest that would feed the deer and rabbits and pheasants they would later hunt.

Yard work. The day of the dynamite could be summed up with those two prosaic words.

I knew from my own yard in Virginia what could happen when old stumps remained. The dead wood and roots would rot, at first pocking the ground with small holes. Later, the dirt would sink and crater. We'd find a small animal skull in one. We'd trip and almost twist an ankle, falling into another. We'd finally have to pay for a dump truck of dirt to plug up all the damage of those festering suckers, the ones that should have been removed from the ground as soon as the tree died and was cut down.

Those remnants left behind, those pieces of the past. I hadn't realized ignoring them could create a sinkhole.

I thought I knew something about this accident. But, as Barry said, you need to do your research to know the reality.

I had imagined a Vietnam War protest. Or a scheme to dodge the draft. A political statement. I thought he might be a hero or a rebel, I wasn't sure which, but either way he was doing something bigger than I could have understood as a child, which is why no one had ever offered an explanation. Something warlike or peaceful but surely grandiose and complex.

My father was only blowing up tree stumps—what they called suckers. Barry was the one who discovered they could bore into the snow with a broom, drop some dynamite in, and make a hole in the ground.

Barry had cautioned my father. Who knows how Barry caught a glimpse into the future, but he did, and my father still held on tight to the dynamite. Only he could tell me why.

No wonder this story seemed mythic to me. The voice Barry heard could have come from the gods, descending to Earth. Or from God.

Playing with dynamite? It's the word *play* that tripped me up, the word I'd heard all my life. That word had conjured up boy-men goofing off, horsing around, a bunch of daredevil kids on the prowl for cheap stimulation, trying to see what they could get away with, pumping their adrenaline for the sheer joyride of it. I hadn't realized I'd been looking back on my father and shaking my head at him, as if he were one of my wayward children.

But he had been working, not playing, like my grandfather before him and my uncle now, acting as caretakers of the land. What a relief I should have felt. And yet. I wasn't ready to give up my stories.

CORA SAID, "TELL HER WHY it blew up."

"I found out only *years* later," Barry said. "When I was in Vietnam, I was a nuclear demolition specialist, but I was cross-trained on conventional demos. In the training school they told us the military rarely shoots with a fuse, they usually shoot electrically. But if we did have to shoot with a fuse we should always cut some fuse off the spool and throw it away before we cut the next piece we were going to use. If you haven't cut anything off the fuse in the last ten minutes or more, you need to cut fourteen inches off it and throw that away, because you can get a runner."

"A runner?" I asked.

"A dynamite fuse burns a ring. You can see right where it's at when it burns, as it goes through. It smokes and blows fire out of it. It's made up of fine stranded string. I don't know what it's got in it but it burns. A runner is when one of those strings is lit but you don't see it."

"The fuse is lit but you can't see that it's lit," Cora explained.

Barry said, "That's what got Jerry. There was a runner. He was holding the dynamite and the fire was burning right down the fuse, but it didn't look like it was. The fuse was showing that the fire had hardly moved down at all, but it was actually way ahead of where it looked."

But why did he hold the dynamite in his hand at all? Couldn't he have placed it in the ground and lit it after?

I wanted to protect this vulnerable teenager with his hand on fire. Of course, I had an unfair advantage, gazing at my teenage father through a maternal lens. If he had lived to his forties like me, he could have become more cautious, as I did. He would have, I wanted to believe, so much that my shoulders and chest and teeth clenched, as if I were praying for the hypothetical future of a nineteen-year-old who looks like me and seemed, at that moment, more like my son than my father.

I sat paralyzed on the couch, sinking in the plush. *I believe I have lost my . . .* what? What did *I* lose? Some of the stories I'd told myself. Maybe even my secret wish that my father's past was darker, more exciting and dramatic than it really was, which might mean my life was more meaningful and exceptional.

"And then there was this other big deal," Barry said. "I don't know if I ever told you."

I pivoted forward. My ears practically in his mouth.

Barry rose from his chair and paced. "I was in Jerry's hospital room, he was asleep, and the doctors had just told me what they did to treat him. Then a huge guy came in. He looked like a bouncer. This is part of why I hate cops so bad."

I flinched.

"The guy was about six foot six in a big brown suit. I can see his face, like he's standing right here in front of me. He grabbed me by my shirt and said, 'Are you his brother?' I said, 'Yeah,' and he said, 'You come with me,' and he led me by my collar. He grabbed Dave in the hall, walked up to the counter by the nurse's station and said, 'I'm going in that doctor's conference room. I don't want to be disturbed.'"

"Who was he?" I asked.

"He was the FBI."

My knees squeezed. My shoulders stiffened. I felt time suspend. Whatever my uncle said in the next five minutes might finally make the past intelligible.

"Wow." That's all I said, one word. Me, the English major. I don't know how anything works—cars or guns or explosives. But words are supposed to be easy. I should be able to convey the largeness of this story, instead of expressing myself monosyllabically.

Barry said, "He flapped his badge. He threatened me and wanted to know where we got all this stuff, and what we'd been doing with it. I said, 'What is this all about?' But he wouldn't tell me. I was only seventeen. He grabbed me out of my chair and shook me." Barry curled his hands around two invisible shoulders and shook the air.

"Disgusting," I said.

"Yeah. True police brutality. Dave had just slipped off into one of his dazes. The agent asked Dave something but then wouldn't let him finish. The guy said, 'What's your name?' Dave said, 'My name is—' then he asked him another question before he could finish his sentence, trying to get a rise out of him, to confuse him, that old police interrogation trick."

Barry leaned back, then gestured with his fist. "The guy doubled up like he was going to hit me in the face, and I said, 'I'm not going to say another damn word to you until you tell me what this is all about.' Then everything calmed down. We sat there. It seemed like hours but it was probably a minute. Finally, he said, 'All right, we know you were in Camp Grayling today.' We were. How he knew that I don't know. We just drove through it."

"Cameras," Cora said.

"Back then?" Barry asked. "Anyway, he said, 'Dynamite was stolen from Camp Grayling.'"

"A military base," Cora explained.

"And I said 'I got a receipt for that dynamite. I got proof that I bought it.' Everything changed after that. His whole demeanor."

"They thought you stole it?" I asked.

"Yeah. He called the sheriff in Kalkaska and the sheriff was sitting there when we came home at about three in the morning. I gave the sheriff the dynamite with the receipt and everything to prove it. My dad, he was so screwed up he wanted to go get the dynamite back. And I said, 'Oh my God, I don't want it.'"

So that was it. No Weathermen. No political underground, criminal activity, or civil disobedience. Oh my God. But I didn't say that. I didn't say anything. I turned off the tape and let my uncle's words sink in.

That was the story, the story I'd come for. Or was it?

Something was missing. I didn't know what, and I didn't know how I knew. I got a funny feeling. You could call it a premonition. Or, to use Barry's earlier words, "you could just call it knowledge of what *could* happen."

But life is full of bad things waiting to catch us off guard, disasters narrowly averted or not at all. My father knew that as well as I did.

Lighting explosives can be risky. But so is walking your dog or traveling across town. I understood from my uncle's story that the world is a dangerous place unless we stay home and lock the door. I like to think my father would understand why I was unwilling to do that. After my uncle paused, I remembered a few times when I had also been in danger. I wished I could share these snippets with my father, then reassure him that now I was all right.

Snippets like these. At fourteen I started riding the Detroit city bus alone and walking the mile home from Outer Drive, after the suburban line near my house stopped running for the night. This was Detroit in the eighties, after the manufacturing jobs moved out but before the hipsters moved in. I was at my most vulnerable, a nubile morsel, stalked and harassed and cat-called by how many men? I couldn't keep count.

I was living the life of a girl too young yet to drive, using the tools at my disposal to see and do what I needed to see and do. If my only concern had been safety, I would never have walked out my door at all.

Some people choose that option, of course. No wonder I was drawn to agoraphobes.

A strange thing happened as I slipped into my father's teenage head. From the outside, all I could see were our differences. But, through his eyes, I saw my own risky youth.

I saw myself as a high school freshman disguised as a college student—tight dark jeans, chunky black boots with metal hardware, vintage canvas shirt, all from the Salvation Army, all with a wink at 1940s glamour and 1980s irony. One day I wandered the Detroit Institute of Arts alone, staring at the engravings of Adam and Eve I knew so well. A group of college boys, their gaunt bodies and wavy hair reminding me of Adam himself, broke my trance. "We've been watching you," one of them said.

The other grinned and added, "We've been stalking you."

"For hours," said the third.

"You're so intense," said the fourth.

"The museum's about to close," said my favorite, the one with the scrub of facial hair at the bottom of his chin like a comma, "you must be hungry."

He probably heard my stomach growling. I hadn't eaten since breakfast, since I couldn't afford to buy lunch out. They lived across the street, they said, on the Wayne State campus. They'd make me spaghetti. "Come on," the one with the Ramones T-shirt said then grabbed my arm.

Should I have allowed four men I'd known five minutes to corral me into a private room, where no one would see what they did to me (four on one, when even one could pin me down)? Four men who had admitted to stalking me. The spaghetti was hot and spicy. Nothing bad happened that night, but it could have.

AT NINETEEN, I SLAMMED THE airport taxi door so hard I almost smashed my thumb, then walked out into the dark, starry, silent night of a city I'd never visited before.

I was wearing nothing but a tank top and slippery-mermaid-tight jeans. I seemed to walk right into the horizon, it loomed so large, a cowboy Colorado sky graced by the most formidable mountains I'd ever seen. The *only* mountains I'd ever seen. I didn't have a bed. I didn't have a phone. I didn't have a clue.

I marched purposefully ("Always look like you know where you're going, even if you don't" all the self-defense books I'd devoured at the library advised me) to the office where I was supposed to retrieve my dorm key. Closed. All the doors on the campus of what was then called the Naropa School of Disembodied Poetics, in Boulder, were locked and dark. I knocked on every door and window. "Hello! Anybody there?" Even the library stood empty. The dorms must be somewhere on campus, I figured. If I could find them, someone would wake up and let me in.

I'd bought the cheapest flight I could find from New York City (using borrowed money from my grandparents), on a no-frills airline that longer exists and was, of course, hugely delayed. I'd won a scholarship to study poetry for a month the summer after sophomore year in a program co-run by my idol, Beatnik poet Allen Ginsberg. Allen Ginsberg of *Howl* fame. Allen Ginsberg, who wrote, "I saw the best minds of my generation destroyed by madness, starving hysterical naked, / dragging themselves through the negro streets at dawn looking for an angry fix, / angelheaded hipsters burning for the ancient heavenly connection to the starry dynamo in the machinery of night." *That* Allen Ginsberg.

I swirled around in my own machinery of night. I was too hungry to think straight, my last meal in my apartment at noon. I wasn't quite starving, wasn't quite hysterical, wasn't quite naked. But almost. The sound of leaves crunching (not the pattering of a chipmunk but the thunking of boots) made me slow my breath and still my body. ("If you run, someone might chase you; if you will yourself to become invisible, he might not see you," the self-defense books also said). Why had I practically sprayed on my jeans? How had I not seen this coming?

I tiptoed, soundless, to the edge of campus, the sidewalk, then the street. ("If you're alone at night, find the lights. If you think you're being followed, walk in the road against traffic. You want him to worry he'll be *seen*.") I could do this until I came to a pay phone. Then what? Whom could I call?

The cool mountain air chilled the sweat on my bare shoulders. I shivered.

New York City always made me feel safe. All those lights, all those people; whatever happened, someone would *see* it happen, right? But here there was hardly a car. This was hippie town, I'd been told, which was true, judging by the smattering of Volkswagen buses and beetles. A red Bug stopped at my right and rolled down the window. A middle-aged man with dark sideburns shouted, "Are you lost?"

I'd been gazing straight ahead, shoulders back, head up, the way the books told me to look when I wanted to fool people into thinking I knew where I was going. I shook my head and kept walking. He cruised alongside me, the instructions for retrieving my dorm key fluttering in my hand. "Get in," he said, in an accent I couldn't place. And, against all advice I'd heard about stranger danger since I was four years old, I did.

He told me he taught at the University of Colorado. I didn't ask why he was cruising the streets in the middle of the night. I just slept on his couch.

The next morning, he dropped me off at the Naropa office and asked me to meet him for a movie at seven o'clock. The request felt like a command. I owed him something for his hospitality, but I didn't want to go on a date. I had a boyfriend, and, besides, my host was twice my age.

I met him anyway. In the dark on-campus theater, the Japanese film began in a teahouse. Geishas from another century or millennium served long-haired top-knotted men with swords. Hardly past the credits, their clothes were off. I felt a squeeze on my bare knee. Then fingers trailing under my skirt. I didn't owe him that much, did I?

I rose to leave, but he clamped me down with his arm. Here we were again, in the dark. I wasn't *that* kind of girl. The kind of girl who entered strangers' cars. OK, I was.

I didn't want to hurt his feelings. He had been so kind. But if he could hold me down in my seat, what else might he do, in the privacy of his car or apartment? Finally, with a burst of adrenaline, I pulled my body upright and ran out of the theater; out of the lush, green, fertile campus; down the street; past angelheaded hipsters burning for the ancient heavenly connection; past Celestial Seasonings-drinking, pot-smoking, bead-wearing long hairs. Back to my dorm.

THE INVENTOR OF DYNAMITE HIMSELF was a paradox. Alfred Nobel created the most destructive tool of his day and yet he considered himself a pacifist. When he died, he left behind a $9 million endowment to award people whose work helps humanity. The history of dynamite is about money, power, and prestige. It's about peace and progress. It's about much more than blowing things up.

My father lost his right hand the day he held that stick of dynamite and didn't let go. Of course, there was more to the story.

But for now, let's leave him dangling in the hospital, about to wake up and discover the eerie sensation of having a phantom limb. Let him drift off for a few more hours before he tries to pound his forehead against a missing palm, then starts the formidable task of relearning how to shoot and eat and write and drive and weld, all with his left, nondominant hand. Let's backtrack.

Who was he before I met him? What kind of boy? What kind of young man? I'd been at Barry and Cora's house little more than an hour and already I'd learned more about my father than I had over decades of my adulthood, when I couldn't bring myself to even ask the right questions. We sank deeper into the furniture. Cora refilled our mugs and tucked an afghan over my lap. I didn't realize I'd been shivering.

"My parents were so damn strict." That's what Barry told me in his living room my first night at his house. "Ma and Dad never let Jerry and me do nothing."

Then he launched into a story.

When my father and Barry were ten and twelve, their parents spent the weekends Up North and the work weeks Downstate, but they'd let the boys stay in the country while they returned to work in the city, as a pipefitter and nurse's aide. My great-grandparents lived a mile away but the boys were old enough to stay by themselves.

For the setting of the story, I filled in my own memories of that house Up North. I'd been told that when my grandparents married, my grandfather's parents gave him a parcel of land near the farm where he grew up, and he started to build a house. When the Second World War broke out he abandoned the project and moved to the city for work. The house lacked plumbing and electricity, the only heat came from a potbellied stove in the living room and the wood burning stove in the adjacent kitchen. The entryway was lined with coal and wood for fuel, and the kitchen walls were penciled with records of fish that my father and Uncle Barry had caught in the 1950s. The walls of the kitchen were covered, almost from floor to ceiling, with *Playboy* calendars from every year, going back to at least the 1960s. There were almost no doors on the interior; all the doorways except the one leading to the second floor were closed off by curtains. But in many ways it was better than any other shelter. It was magical, like a treehouse. Staying in it felt like camping. Sleeping in it was like sleeping under the sky. It blended in with the woods.

IF I SQUINT, I CAN see my father and uncle in that same house. I imagine it like this.

The two brothers, their voices cracking with the promise of a deeper boom to come, climb into the red Pontiac, its seats covered with pristine towels, at four in the morning, and sleep till they arrive at the road with our family name, near the town of Kalkaska. Alma and Kenneth, their parents, carry in the house a paper grocery bag full of nonperishables: powdered milk and cereal, raisins, peanut butter, jelly, bread, and a dozen tins of the kippers the boys both love so much.

Then they drive down the road to the "stone house," where the boys' grandparents live, constructed of large colored stones embedded in cement. They fill coolers from the well. George, their grandfather, ambles out to meet them.

"Getting rid of the varmints for a few days?" George asks, joking as usual.

"We'll pick them up in a week," Kenneth says. "They'll stay up at our house by themselves. Won't be no trouble to you, just need to use your well is all."

"Don't run me dry, boys," George jokes. "And stay away from my chickens."

"You think they're damn dogs?" Kenneth jokes back. George's feisty old barn cat whips her tail to taunt them.

"We brought our own food," my father says.

"You get sick of peanut butter, just remember. You got to go to church if you want Sunday supper. See you here at 9:30 sharp. I expect you to be spit clean." His voice teasing. Of course they'd go to church. They always did.

They use the outhouse at midnight by themselves, on the lookout for cougars, raccoons, or bears. They don't need adult supervision. They don't have faucets or lights. They don't have phones or toilets or any water but what's in the coolers from the well. They have all they need. And they've got guns.

As soon as the Pontiac recedes, a red splatter on the horizon like a sunset, they pull out their shotguns, something their parents don't let them do in the house when they're around.

In the dead of summer it's hunting season for nothing. They could carry a gun in the woods in case a cougar comes pounding out of a tree. But those animals are too elusive. Something stirs. They can blast the mice.

My father lifts his twenty-gauge and prowls. He hears mice from down in the basement so he cuts up some shotgun shells, dumps out most of the powder, then shoves a wad of paper in. He thrusts the shortened shell into the rifle and crouches down to the floorboards. The house doesn't have planks yet, as it did when I used to stay there. It just has a subfloor, plywood sheets with open space between them.

A short shotgun shell won't travel far. My father calibrates its length to be just enough to hit a mouse but not to gouge a hole in the dirt bottom of the basement.

"I dare you to shoot the living room floor," my father says.

"What if I hit a can of gas or something? Blow the place up?" his brother asks.

"Chicken!" my father teases. "I'll show you who's the man of this house. The king of this castle."

Bam! Bam! Bam! He shoots them up. The mice squeak then they squeak no more. It's better than pinball.

"I STILL HAVE THE CAR we used to drive up there," Barry said.

"You drove when you were ten?"

"It wasn't nothing but a Model A. Wouldn't go that fast."

"Was that legal?"

"A cop stopped me once, said 'Show me your license.' 'I ain't got no license,' I said. 'I know you ain't, you little son of a bitch,' he said. 'Don't let me catch you again.'" Barry chuckled. "Taught me to stay away from the cops is all." The rules in the country are not the same as rules in the city, he explained. A slow car on a remote back road can't do much harm. But still.

The only light in the unfinished farmhouse was from propane lamps. Knock one over and they would have caught the wooden house on fire. To cook, you had to light a wood-burning stove. So many ways my father could have come to a premature end.

I COULD SAY THE SAME thing about myself.

I spent the summer between my freshman and sophomore years of college living on Detroit's east side with my boyfriend and working in a hospital in the middle of the Cass Corridor. I didn't own a car, so during the one-week city bus strike, I had to walk part of the way to work. I could walk to a bus stop for the suburban bus, which would take me downtown. Then I had to walk from there, past drug dealers leaning against pay phones outside blood banks, past abandoned houses, past bars with blow-up gorillas on their signs and plastic trash bags on their windows. One morning I was followed, and I ran a mile up Woodward Avenue, searching every storefront for an Open sign or a light on and finding none, finally arriving in my hospital oasis dripping with sweat.

Was this the common currency I shared with my father—the frequency with which we allowed ourselves to flirt with danger? I was trying hard to find something to connect us.

My father's risks—shooting and speeding and lighting explosives in the woods—seem to be born of bravado and machismo. His dangers were foreign to me. Would mine have seemed foreign to him?

I wanted to see indie films and work summer and afterschool jobs in a city that could be dangerous for girls on foot. I wanted to take the bus to art exhibits and readings and poetry classes and performances. I didn't want anyone to tell me I couldn't do what I wanted to do just because I was a girl. If I'd worried too much about keeping safe, where would that have taken me? I wouldn't have even been able to walk my dog.

ONE SUMMER AFTERNOON WHEN I was twelve, I led Excalibur a couple miles from home and we ended up under the viaduct where I-75 crossed above our heads. It was so dark under the metal bridge that I didn't see a man lurking against the wall.

My beagle didn't bark or lunge or bite. He didn't do squat.

The man pinned my shoulders and pointed a knife to my neck. He was lanky and scruffy, mid-twenties maybe. He laughed, and I was sure I was going to die after he did whatever he was going to do to me first.

I froze. If I didn't move, maybe I could pretend this wasn't happening.

And then it wasn't. He pocketed the knife, slicked back his hair, and laughed again, this time with fake intimacy. "I was just kidding," he said. "Can't you take a joke?" His arms wandered over my shoulders.

I still said nothing, careful not to break the spell of his new, light mood. I walked with him for a mile or so, even after he let go, past Taco Bell and Hardee's, past Burger King and Arby's. If I didn't have my dog, perhaps I would have rushed inside and asked someone to call the police. But all I could think was *Dogs aren't allowed in restaurants.*

I walked beside this creep, his arm around my shoulders or my waist, his knife jingling in his pocket, wondering if he would change his mind and pin me down again, till he turned right and let me turn left. I ran the three blocks home from there, but I didn't call the police. I told no one.

It's hard to remember why I was silent. Maybe I was afraid I wouldn't be believed.

Maybe I didn't want people to tell me the world was too dangerous for girls to navigate alone.

Two years after I met Knife Man, I was attacked a second time, walking home from a high school play. Three blocks from my house, someone jumped out of the alley and followed me. I race-walked because the self-defense books I'd read since my first attack said, "If you run, he'll chase you."

Only one block from my house, he pushed me down on the cement and ripped off my clothes. Then I remembered another piece of self-defense advice. "Pretend you know him."

"George!" I said. "Don't you remember me?" I made up a slew of details, as if the more specific I was, the more believable I sounded.

Maybe his name really was George. Or maybe the way I looked him in the eye made him fear I could (and would) identify him to the police. Abruptly (and miraculously, it seemed at the time), he fled.

As I sat on my aunt and uncle's couch, these scenes resurfaced. I didn't like to remember the times I'd been in danger. So why was I doing so now? Perhaps I needed to be reminded why my father had wanted to teach us kids to be tough.

I drank more coffee, ate more Kit Kats, and leaned back, listening to my uncle bring to life the boy my father used to be. I tried to imagine what my hometown was like back then. As my mother had said in Paris, if I wanted to understand him I had to put him in context. If he was a man of his time, he must have also been a man of his place.

THE DETROIT OF HIS CHILDHOOD is not the same as the Detroit of mine. Or the Detroit today. With every breath we take, more teachers lose their jobs, more water gets shut off, more lawns turn to weeds then back to forest. The population declines, and the once-brimming streets risk ghost town status.

Suburbanites don't venture into the city much these days, except for a ball game. Most people don't even work downtown anymore, the offices scattered in suburbs like Southfield or Pontiac or Livonia.

Detroit in the 1950s, when my father was young, is the Detroit I want to imagine. This was the city in its age of innocence, before the riots that tore it apart.

The year I was born was the year Detroit started to die. During the long, hot summer of 1967, the city erupted in one of the deadliest riots in the nation's history. Sparked by a police raid on an unlicensed bar, the riots lasted four days and nights, left scores dead and hundreds injured, thousands arrested, hundreds of businesses looted and buildings destroyed. The governor sent in thousands of National Guard troops, and the president ordered paratroopers to keep order. Yet long before calm was restored, chaos reigned. Those who could afford to fled to the suburbs, and housing prices plummeted. Detroit's reputation did too.

In the 1950s and 1960s Detroit had a larger black middle class than most American cities its size—thanks to strong unions, high employment, and the auto industry—but that didn't mean there was racial harmony.

The Detroit of my father's childhood was a seemingly dormant volcano waiting to erupt.

The Mickey Mouse Club was on TV, *I Love Lucy, Bonanza, Gunsmoke*. Men were cowboys or singers, and women were ditzy dames or Mouseketeers. The Hudson's store at Woodward and Gratiot had not yet been demolished and was still the tallest department store in the world (with thirty-two floors) and the second largest in square feet (second only to Macy's in New York City). Assembly line jobs created a robust middle class, and the city was still a place people fled to, not from.

IMAGINE THAT CITY, THAT TIME. Now zero in on one hot and muggy August afternoon at the Michigan State Fair. My uncle started to tell me a story of when my grandmother took the boys there, when they were young, not yet in high school. She used to take me too, so I can easily envision what it was like. The vast space filled with creaky Ferris wheels and carousels, pigs that seemed as big as cows, giant pumpkins, and prizes for quilts and jam. I can taste the funnel cake and corn dogs. I can smell the mix of auto factory spilloff and cow manure. A country affair on the northern edge of the city.

"A guy was selling something," Barry said. "I don't remember what. He had a metal pan, an electrode, and another electrode floating out here." Barry's fingers chopped the air to make these items seem to appear. "He plugged it in and showed that he had 110 flowing into it."

I squinted.

"House current," he explained. "And the guy put his hand in the water." Barry pantomimed the performance of the state fair con man.

"Why?"

"He was trying to show how amazing he was, letting electricity flow through his body. Everybody crowded around, and their eyes went all wide."

My eyes did too, watching him act out the scene.

"Jerry, though, he was just a kid, but he'd been studying chemistry and he knew that pure water don't conduct electricity. You need minerals to do that."

"This guy must've poured distilled water in his pan," Cora said.

"Right," Barry said. "Jerry walked over to a hotdog stand. He grabbed a shaker and dumped the salt in the water. Salt is a good conductor. Needless to say, the guy wasn't about to put his hand in the pan after that."

"The guy had a fit," Cora said. She wasn't there. But she'd heard this story many times.

"He had a *major* fit," Barry said. "Ma wasn't so tickled neither, but she was used to him showing off how he knew more than everybody else."

My mother's words echoed in my head, the ones she'd told me in Paris the previous spring, but also all through my life: My father was the smartest man she ever met.

I DIDN'T THINK OF MYSELF as a smart kid, not compared to my brother, the prodigy. But maybe I was. I like to think so. That's another way I could connect with my father.

I felt smart when I was fourteen and the director of the poetry program at the Detroit Institute of Arts made an exception and allowed me to enroll in classes for adults. My teachers introduced me to William Blake and Frank O'Hara and William Carlos Williams. They taught me how to enter a poem intuitively, to appreciate the sensuality of language. My fellow students—including one who later became an author and *New Yorker* contributor—gave me an intellectual peer group to belong to.

I rode the bus to class every Saturday morning (and when I couldn't afford to pay, a kindly octogenarian who said she'd known Gertrude Stein in Paris offered me a private "scholarship") and to readings the first Saturday night of every month. Paul Auster read. Bernadette Mayer. Alice Notley. My heroes.

One Saturday my brother didn't accompany me. This was the year he spent in New York City, enrolled in a special program for young, gifted students who could earn a college degree before graduating from high school.

A man I didn't know (but who seemed to know me) asked if I wanted to "grab a bite to eat" before the reading. Why not? He was well groomed and polite, oh-so Birmingham and Royal Oak. How much older than me—twenty years? He spoke in full sentences, full paragraphs even, the way I was trying to learn to do. He could teach me a lot, I was sure. We ate fast-food hamburgers with sautéed mushrooms then walked the campus slowly, slowly, finding shade and trees and finally settling on a secluded blanket of grass. "Read me one of your poems," he said. I leaned over to pull the page from my book bag and he took the opportunity to rub against me. I should have seen it coming. I should have told him off. Instead, I just pulled away and said nothing.

I imagined I must have given him signs. I figured I deserved this attention. I couldn't embarrass him by pointing out what he was doing. I thought I had to pretend nothing was happening. Just as I had done, walking beside Knife Man.

These are stories I don't want to remember. We don't talk about such things. I always thought it was my father's early death that made me quiet, but maybe these secret stories did too. I thought if I ignored them, they would go away. I should know by now that secrets can grow so big they crowd out so much else. Family closeness. The possibility for intimacy.

Is it any wonder I learned to crumple into corners? That's what hamsters and rabbits do, creatures who know they are prey. Even after I've grown older and wiser, it can be hard to break the habit of making myself small. A habit I've been practicing for decades.

"CLOSE THE DOOR," MY BOSS said.

I was in my early twenties by this time, working as an editor, producing textbooks and research journals for special education teachers and rehabilitation specialists, rising in rank and responsibility from assistant to associate to managing editor. I never turned down a challenge, worked harder than two people, and was a stickler for keeping on schedule and catching mistakes. I expected to keep climbing.

"I'd like to give you a positive evaluation this year." My boss, in a tweed jacket with corduroy patches as if he were dressed in a Halloween costume as a professor, leaned back in his chair. "I have nothing to fault you for. Except one thing."

I stared at my pumps. I slumped. I nodded and held back the urge to cry. Of course he was right. Whatever he would say was wrong about me was right, I was already sure. "I'm sorry."

"Don't you want to know what you're supposed to be sorry for?"

"Oh. Yes. Sorry."

My boss shook his head. "This is what I mean. Your work is excellent but you don't believe it. You let everyone walk all over you." I didn't think he knew about the "Southern gentlemen" authors I'd allowed to sexually harass me on the phone and at conferences. "If you want to succeed, you need to take some assertiveness training."

AUNT CORA STARTED MAKING DINNER. I could smell the pork roast and home-canned beans and hear the cork pop from the bottle of wine. My aunt and uncle didn't drink, but they'd chilled a bottle just for me.

My father had had to stand up for himself as a man with one hand, or he would never have been offered any jobs at all. Maybe if he had lived, he would have taught me to assert myself. Maybe he still could.

Maybe he could do anything. Wasn't my uncle telling me, again, how supernaturally smart he was? I turned the tape recorder back on.

"At the high school," Barry said, "my teachers were so excited to have me in their classes, Jerry being teacher's pet and all, Jerry being best student in the school, they thought for sure I'd take after him. They weren't so happy, once they saw I wasn't cut out of the same cloth, brain wise. 'We thought you were gonna be a whiz kid like your brother,' they'd say to me.' 'No, I ain't my brother in that way,' I'd say. 'Nobody is.'"

Except my own brother. Maybe he's the one, not me, who really takes after our father.

"Her brother is the smart one," I always figured my teachers said to each other, wishing I could be more like him. What would I do if I lost my brother, the way Barry did? I'd want to tell stories about him. I'd want to do what my uncle was doing, with me, in his living room, regaling us by the fire.

I was trying so hard to identify with my father. But here I was, feeling much more like my uncle.

When I was in high school, I told my mother I was moving to New York City. But even I didn't believe I really could. Someone else did, though. My French teacher.

Everyone deserves a Madame Hausermann. Elfin and elegant, like a red-headed Joan Didion, but with a silk scarf over her shoulders and pointed heels clicking on the school's industrial tile. She drove me to Ann Arbor to help me imagine myself on a college campus. She introduced me to a former student, a Barnard graduate, who warned me of "culture shock" once I got there.

Did she really think I'd ever get there?

I didn't know much about admissions or tuition. All I knew was that Manhattan was where "the writers" lived. At least most of the poets who read in the monthly series at the Detroit Institute of Arts, which was what I cared about most in the world. I applied to only two colleges, both in Manhattan. I had no backup plan, assuming I would be granted a full scholarship or financial aid package.

I can't believe, given the odds, how lucky I was. Both colleges accepted me, with funding.

I'd never felt smarter than the moment I opened those letters, beckoning me to New York City, welcoming me, I assumed, to the center of the literary world.

Maybe one day, I imagined, opening those letters, I could teach too. I could be for someone else what Madame Hausermann had been for me.

"You're too quiet," my friends said. "Your students would walk all over you."

Which was likely true. At least then.

I FELT SMART TOO, THE summer I worked for two doctors after my freshman year of college. I was a temporary secretary for two pioneering AIDS researchers at the Wayne State University medical complex. At first, all they did when they walked past my desk to reach their offices was hand me the tapes they had recorded, so I could listen on the Dictaphone and transcribe them. They were polite but short and businesslike. I had worked as a temporary secretary before and didn't expect my bosses to engage with me socially. I was there to do the monotonous work they didn't have time for.

Then one day, everything changed. One of the doctors asked me what I did before this job. When I told him I was a student, he leaned in. When I said I was at Barnard, part of Columbia University, his whole face opened up. He sat down in my visitor's chair and transformed from a harried employer with no time for niceties to an avuncular peer.

Now he saw me as someone in his own social class. I could be his daughter. I could be his younger self.

He asked what I was studying, and I told him I wanted to be a writer. Miraculously, as soon as I did, he believed I knew how to write. After that, he gave me his research papers to edit. "I should make you my co-author," he joked.

Every day that summer I came to work convinced he'd find me out. "You're no writer," he'd say. "You're just a secretary."

Then every day, when he didn't blow my cover, I boarded the bus home, thinking that maybe his faith in me was not misplaced. Maybe I was smart.

Like my father.

I DON'T USUALLY ASSOCIATE MYSELF with bravado and bluff. I'm the nice one. But, of course, whether I'm the nice one or the smart one depends on which events I remember.

After that summer in Detroit, I had vowed to never live there again. I looked with immature teen-aged condescension on all those who stayed behind.

This is the story I told my new friends in New York City: "I come from a land of drive-in everything—drive-in movies, drive-in beer stores, drive-in banks. The next new thing will be drive-in church and drive-in bowling. Oh, you thought those were two separate windows?"

Was I smart? Or a smart ass? Maybe even, sometimes, an asshole.

Maybe I imagined I was just like Odysseus. After duping the Cyclops, son of Poseidon, he shouted from his ship as he escaped his death, "Fame will remember my name: I, Odysseus was the one who tricked you." The Cyclops told his father to storm the seas and crash the trickster's ship. Had he not indulged his smart ass side, how many years would he have saved, struggling to find the shores of home?

How many years would I have saved too?

BUT NOW I WAS HERE, listening to my uncle say, "My brother in one word is this—intelligent."

I wanted to know my father well enough to say the same thing. I wanted to see him in action, to watch him display his photographic memory, his debating skills, his analytical wizardry. I wanted to witness him dazzling and devastating his peers from church.

Barry told me about the day the youth group from Glenwood Methodist rang the bell, trying to talk my father into joining. He did *not* want to, but my grandfather said they had to let them in.

I wasn't born when that youth group arrived on their doorstep. But this story sounded familiar, like a tale I'd grown up with. Maybe my father had told me himself, which is why I felt as if I were there, in his head.

I imagined the scene this way.

LIKE ME AT MY HALF-ADULT/half-child stage, my father has bright red hair and freckles galore. Too muscled to be called skinny, too wiry to be big. More fox than wolf, his shoulders yet to widen with hard work. His face is a smooth and angular oval except for the red mustache he started growing at thirteen, tinder for the constant blow-ups with his father.

His mouth is screwed up into a sneer which, when frozen in a photograph, looks menacing. In person and in motion, though, the way he curls his lips is just mischievous.

His hair is a little wavy and slicked back with grease. He is wearing jeans and penny loafers, a pullover with a casual shirt from JCPenney down the street. Teenage Barry's dressed the same as his brother. Barry would never grow a mustache, though, even if he could at thirteen. It's not worth the fight, he tells my father all the time.

Barry is so much smaller, people don't usually believe he's just a year younger than his brother. He hasn't had his growth spurt yet, hasn't sprouted hair, even on his chest. My father calls him "girl" as an insult, and Barry laughs and calls him "bearded lady."

Their house is a cozy one-story brick. A kitchen just big enough to fit a Formica table, a living room, bathroom, and two bedrooms. A basement with a dining room table used for holiday meals. The house is much smaller now, in my head, than it seemed to me as a child.

My father and Barry sprawl across their beds, with matching red corduroy tasseled spreads. Above my father's bed he's taped magazine pictures of Bob Dylan and Johnny Cash and James Dean. On Barry's side hangs a rabbit's foot from an animal he caught and skinned and ate and a picture of the high school girls synchronized swim team, in their bright blue and orange suits, cut out of the local paper, *The Mellus*. Barry messes with an alarm clock he took apart for kicks and is trying to reassemble. My father, as usual, is in a reading trance. He's so absorbed he's deaf.

"Jerry!" my grandfather yells, then walks into the bedroom and plucks the *Reader's Digest* from my father's eyes. "Don't tell me you can't hear. I've been shouting at you so long your goddamn mustache grew three inches. Can't you hear the doorbell? There's some kids here to see you."

My grandfather pulls my father upright. "Answer the damn door!"

My father does. The girls wear clingy short sleeve sweaters, pencil skirts, and loafers with white socks. The boys sport sweater vests and squeaky shined shoes.

The small, shy, blonde girl reminds my father of a canary. The other girl is trying too hard, wearing a pointy bra that makes her look like a torpedo. Canary's the kind my father likes, the type of girl he wants to marry someday.

My father waves in the girls, as well as a boy in a cardigan and another with a buzz cut. Canary, Torpedo, Cardigan, and Buzz.

"Have a seat. I'll turn off Walter Cronkite because I have you people here to tell me The Good News." Jerry laughs at his pun, and so does Barry, but the youth group steal glances at each other. He says "Good News" in a voice that is half evangelical preacher, half game show emcee.

My father takes ownership of the vinyl rocker/recliner. Barry moves an ottoman in front of the TV and offers the youth group the sofa and the armchair.

"Tea and cookies, ladies?" my father asks the whole group.

"Sure," the two girls say.

My father shrugs in a grand gesture that says, Couldn't you tell I was kidding?

"Speaking of cookies," Cardigan says, "our youth group is having a progressive dinner this Friday night. You go from house to house for different courses. Mine is dessert. My mom makes the best chocolate chip cookies on the planet."

"OK, I'll join your group," my father says.

Cardigan elbows Torpedo with I-told-you-so swagger.

"If you can answer me just a few basic questions about theology." My father starts with a list of Old Testament contradictions. He quotes Leviticus, the verses about the godliness of polygamy and the sinful nature of eating shrimps. He quotes Genesis and asks how the world could have literally been created in seven days when you look at biological facts and the laws of physics, which he details.

Buzz, silent until that moment, points his finger toward heaven and rebuts my father's claims by saying the New Testament supersedes the Old so those rules no longer apply. The group starts to gloat, Torpedo thrusting out her pointy breasts.

Then my father wiggles his mustache and starts in on the New Testament. "Why do the four gospels contradict each other?"

"They don't," Cardigan says, rolling up his sleeves for a verbal fight.

All four in the group noticeably droop when my father quotes God's word at odds with itself. He knows more scripture than they do. He's a machine. How can they compete? He's like one of those slick city attorneys on TV who could convince a jury that Mother Teresa should go to jail.

My father brings Thomas Paine and Friedrich Nietzsche

into the discussion, quoting *The Age of Reason* and *Thus Spake Zarathustra*. The group is afraid to say they don't know who these authors are. Did they miss something in Sunday school? Clearly, he tells them, anybody with any sense can see they've all been duped. Even Canary starts to squirm.

Fourteen. The age of reason, or at least the age of constant questioning and intellectual crisis. The age I was when I stopped attending church regularly, changing my vocational goal from missionary in Africa to writer in New York City. I'd started working at A&W, especially requesting Sundays. When I ran into members of my church youth group, I'd say I had to work. That I needed the money. But really I was running away from God.

My Sunday School teachers that year were Lola and Billy, a cute young couple not much older than the teens they taught. Lola flipped her long dark hair and wore short dresses I coveted, clothes that made her look hip. Billy played guitar, he kept telling us, as if we'd believe him more if we thought he was like the MTV stars we worshipped.

I attended a Free Methodist Church, not an Evangelical one, but Billy and Lola believed that every word in the Bible was God's literal truth. One Sunday morning I asked about evolution. "That's blasphemy," Billy said. "You know God created the world in seven days. It didn't take millions of years for man to walk on earth."

"But what about dinosaurs?" I asked. "How do you explain them?"

"They didn't exist," Lola said.

"They're in the *Encyclopedia Britannica*." I spent countless hours after school reading through random entries in the library.

"They're fakes," she said.

No, you are. I said that only to myself, but I left the room and sat outside till Sunday School was over.

THE SUN MOVED DOWN THE horizon out the wall-size picture windows. I could almost see my father inching closer and closer. "Tell her about Groner," Cora said.

I couldn't get over how much my aunt remembered. She's related to my father only by marriage, but she knows him so much better than I do. She has even memorized his childhood and could prompt Barry's memory. I was the in-law, the outsider, the one who didn't know the family lore.

I heard that Devere Groner was a farm mechanic. He worked on tractors and farm equipment. Barry and my father were Up North at their grandparents' house. Their Uncle Norville was up there too. "He was a real good guy," Barry said, "but he was raised like a woman."

"He was very naive," Cora explained.

Women were naïve?

Barry said, "Norville was six feet something tall, a great big macho man. But he was just . . . I don't know how to describe it." He threw up his hands. "Kinda like a woman."

"He was a gentle soul," Cora said. "He was the kindest man you could ever know. He recited poetry and played guitar."

"They'd worked on a mag needle," Barry said. "It generates a high tension spark to fire a spark plug. You use it instead of a distributor, and it will shock the *shit* out of you. Groner got the mag needle fixed and put it on the tractor, which was sitting there running, perched on top of rubber. He pulled the plug wire off and arced it to the truck."

"Crack! Crack!" Barry opened and closed his hands, imitating explosions with his fingers. "It threw lightning off the engine. Then he touched it and hung onto it. All he was getting was a little bit of shock through the air because the tractor was sitting on rubber. But Uncle Norville, he didn't know that, he just saw the lightning and got all excited. He said, 'Oh my lord, how can you stand that?' He was just *testifying*. Groner laughed. He held onto the tractor and there was another Crack! Crack! Crack! Uncle Norville said, 'Oh my Lord' again.

Barry and Cora laughed at the joke, even though they must have told and heard it a hundred times. I laughed too, but I could almost feel the electric shock sparking my own skin.

Barry demonstrated how my father put his hand on the fender and touched Groner on his earlobe with the other hand. "We heard the electric shock go Crack! Crack! Crack! so bad that Groner fell right to the ground. Uncle Norville damn near shit his pants. Then Jerry, real calm, just told him, 'See, he ain't no tougher than the rest of us. He just didn't have it grounded.' Of course Jerry shocked himself to prove the point. Just as bad as he shocked Groner. The pain had to be incredible. But there was no way he was going to let himself fall to the ground."

I sucked in my teeth. A hissing sound.

"We just all thought it was funny," Barry said. "Of course my folks got mad at him. But he just blew that off."

Yes, my father was a show-off, who enjoyed humiliating someone in public. This story showed the kind of bravado my brother remembered most. But this was also the story of a nephew protecting his beloved Uncle Norville, the gentle soul who couldn't protect himself. Maybe my father, like all of us, was more than one thing at a time. For instance, he wasn't just smart, he could make people laugh. I'd been wrong to think of him as deadly serious.

CORA SWITCHED ON THE LIGHTS, the nights so long that time of year. Barry told me about Bud, a dog they had as kids. Bud was sweet. He'd sometimes hunt, sometimes not. He was a Ferdinand beagle, like the bull who would rather smell the flowers than fight.

The boys' grandpa, my great-grandpa George, had a bunch of old barn cats. "Bud ambled up to an old tom laying in the yard," Barry said, "and that tom promptly whooped his ass and chased him." George laughed and told them they had a wimpy dog. Not wimpy. A *sissy* dog. He liked to tease them about it.

Cora said, "A sissy *city* dog."

"Even worse," I said.

A few years passed and the boys got a beagle named Ex, short for Excalibur. A dog, unlike the beagle Ex I grew up with, who would "kill any creature that got in front of him."

They drove to their grandparents' house Up North, with Ex in the trunk and saw that same old barn cat, the one that used to terrorize Bud, lying out in the yard. Their father said, "Now you kids, don't let that damn dog out of the trunk. We're just going be here for a little bit."

But there was that same damn cat flipping its tail, "just like this." Barry, telling the story, vamped like a cat vaunting its freedom and making fun of a dog stuck in the jail of the trunk.

My father said, "Let's see how Ex does." So they popped the trunk and he took Ex out.

He held him and aimed him at that cat. Ex's eyes changed colors, his ears went back, his hair bristled, his feet dogpaddled in the air. My father said to Ex, "Get him."

They dropped the dog, and the cat jumped up and went "phhttt." The dog threw him in the air, and you could hear stuff crunching. The cat hit the ground.

Then out of the house came old George with his cane. He said, "That dog's going to kill my cat." The boys freed the tom, and the dog promptly cut a big circle out and killed two chickens before they could calm him down.

But first, my father smiled at his grandpa and said, '*This* one's not a sissy city dog—is he?"

My father trained our dog, Excalibur, for hunting.

After my father died, our Ex became a sissy city dog. He dug under the fence and ran away again and again. He raided open trash cans and bounded across busy streets, his floppy ears whooshing behind, his tail wagging even faster than his paws were running. But all we had to do was jump in the car and drive after him, then open the door, and he'd jump right in. We'd drive him to A&W, order him a hamburger without the bun, and he'd lick our faces, up and down, chin to brow, telling us with his lying tongue, that he'd never leave again.

After my father died, I became a sissy city girl. I never learned how to shoot a gun. I never even picked up a crossbow. I couldn't clean a deer. All my meat came from the market. I lived in New York City, for God's sake, and didn't own a car the first ten years. You can't get less country than that.

Maybe if Ex hadn't been a sissy city dog he would have protected me when I was held at knifepoint under the viaduct. Maybe if I hadn't been a sissy city girl, I wouldn't have walked for miles with my attacker, unable to protect myself.

SO MANY DANGERS. MINE AND his. It's hard to believe any of us live to see our children grow up to wag their fingers at us.

In the winter, when their parents went to work, Barry told me that he and my father buried sticks of dynamite in the snow as a practical joke. Their cousin was the first to walk up the path, and a blast of snow hit him like a natural disaster.

They shot cannons in the house and baked gunpowder in the oven. "What did your parents think about that?" I asked.

"Ma wouldn't have been happy," Barry said, "but she was at work."

"Kids," I said, shaking my head. Now that I was a parent myself, I shook my head more often than I meant to.

"I never got into any trouble myself." I meant my tone to be sarcastic, but my wit is often so dry people misread it. As Barry did now.

"I didn't think so," he said.

ONE OF MY NICKNAMES IN middle school was The Nun. I was a goody-goody. That's the story people told about me. But it isn't the whole story.

I DIDN'T HAVE TO CONFESS. But I could see in the lines of his face, the way he clenched his jaw and bit his lip, that he was reaching, straining, grasping to share a kind of truth, and it was only fair for me to do the same with him. So I said, "Did you know I've done LSD?"

Barry folded his body in half, leaning in to hear better. "You're kidding me."

"I was sixteen."

"Now that I find hard to believe."

I told Barry that I never told my mother, but my brother knew. I'd just come home from hearing a band. My boyfriend was a twenty-one-year-old punk rock guitarist and everybody had been passing out tabs of LSD at the gig. My boyfriend dropped me off, and I was up all night, hallucinating. I ate a whole box of Oreos. Louis chewed me out and told me never to take drugs again. He was so mad, but he stayed up all night, taking care of me, anyway.

"That shakes up every idea I ever had about you," Barry said.

I didn't work as a secretary, every summer during college, for nothing. The word, of course, means "keeper of secrets."

The late-fall light was long gone by now. It was time for dinner, then bed. We'd have to wake at dawn the next morning for the long drive. I turned my tape recorder off.

One lesson from my uncle's dynamite story was that premonitions can come true. I wasn't crazy to think mine would, my dread that something bad would happen if I asked about my father's death. Maybe the bad thing was waiting Up North, where I was headed the next day, barring bad weather.

I sucked my pinkie when no one was looking. My fingertips throbbed, red and raw from grinding into them all day.

Part 6
Up North

Overleaf: (*top*) My father's high school graduation, June 1960; (*bottom*)
My high school graduation, June 1985

THE NEXT MORNING, THE SNOW stopped. My alarm went off at five, and I woke in the cozy bedroom my aunt and uncle had prepared for me. The sky remained middle-of-the-night dark as we climbed into the Toyota Camry. My aunt tucked me into the backseat, sweetly, with a blanket. I snuggled into my cocoon, safe and cared for.

I pulled out my phone, not to record this time, but to check the Internet. I read a Facebook post from a friend who lived across the country. In her photo, she wrapped her arms around a woman who resembled her so much she could be her daughter. Because she was.

This was news to me. To all of us on her feed, apparently. She was making an announcement. My friend hadn't seen the girl (who was now a young woman) since she'd given up the baby for adoption, and finally they reconnected. A fairy-tale ending. People don't often share such intimate stories on social media, and I took her post as a gift.

The parallel was striking. Like an adopted child looking for her biological mother, I was searching for a parent I could barely remember. Trying to reconnect with my past. Hoping for my own happily ever after.

THREE HOURS IN, BARRY GASSED up. Bags of sugar beets and apples towered next to the pumps. "Deer food."

We pulled in at The Lumberjack, slipping into a booth decorated like a log cabin. Antlers and feathers hovered over our pancakes and eggs from high exposed rafters.

I didn't turn my recorder on at meals. So we joked about dogs and kids and pit-stops on long-distance road trips. I listened to stories about how much my father liked to hunt pheasants and how the guys he worked with took up a collection for a pheasant sanctuary as a memorial.

If my father had a spirit animal or bird, it would be the pheasant, not the deer, I realized. Cousin to the proud peacock and the immortal phoenix.

With every anecdote the distance shortened between my father and me. I could almost imagine him sitting with us, snug in the booth. He'd be nothing if not opinionated. I wanted to hear him hold forth on politics and books, current events and the latest scientific discoveries. Would he still be the rebel I remembered debating with my grandfather? What would he think of the controversies of our age? Climate change? Immigration? Abortion?

Our unrecorded talk was off the record. Which made this breakfast the perfect time to tell my own family secret. One I'd shared with almost no one.

MONTHS AFTER NOAH WAS BORN, I realized I was trapped in a marriage with an agoraphobic man whose limitations made me feel like I had a second child. A real second child—a sibling for Noah to bond with, as I had with my brother—was out of the question, and I started taking birth control pills. They nauseated me, so my gynecologist recommended Depo Provera, a shot that lasts three months and is 99 percent effective. At my appointment, I took a pregnancy test, waited for the negative result, then rolled up my sleeve for the shot. Three months later, I took the shot without the test. One of the side effects of Depo Provera is a cessation of menses. I hadn't bled for three months.

Then I ballooned. Hormones can make us fat, I knew. I thought this was what it must feel like to not be able to control my weight. I must have been so miserable that I didn't even realize how much I was eating. I thought I'd become one of those people who lose control over their body. I bought bigger clothes.

"Are you pregnant?" my friend Regina asked me in the elevator at work.

"No," I told her, trying to pull in my gut.

I was too tired to think about how to lose weight. I was sure I was developing an ulcer. The twists in my stomach hurt so much, one day I had to go to the doctor. "It's probably indigestion," he said. Noah, just starting to walk, wore me out. I worked full time and took on freelance editing jobs that I started after he went to bed, staying up way past midnight. I paid for a babysitter so Andrew could work on his films during the day, spending money we didn't have. My exhaustion was probably turning me into a hypochondriac. I could have a tumor, I suggested to my doctor, so he sent me to my gynecologist for a sonogram.

I didn't have cancer. I was pregnant.

I cried in the subway as I rushed home to tell Andrew. He responded by saying I couldn't do this to him. That if I had the baby, I would be on my own. That we didn't have enough money.

I told him it might be time to use his trust. His wealthy parents had given him control of a fund when we married. I didn't have access to the account and he had promised me that he was saving it to eventually buy an apartment. This health crisis was more important than real estate. This was an emergency for our emergency money.

But it was gone. He tried to explain, but I couldn't fathom how it was possible to spend so much, more than my annual salary. On what? Rare records and stereo equipment and film supplies? We couldn't even pay our credit card bills, he said.

My body went into shock. Trauma can trigger premature labor. I called a taxi, which rushed me to the emergency room.

The ER doctors injected drugs to halt contractions and told me I had to quit my job and go on bed rest. That was impossible. I was the sole financial support of our family. I was also the main caregiver, to my baby and my husband.

Soon the contractions resumed and I boomeranged back to the hospital. Andrew visited me, leaving Noah with a sitter. "I'm having a panic attack," Andrew told my OB/GYN. "*I* need to be checked into the hospital."

"You're not the patient," my doctor said. But I knew he would always be the patient, whether he wanted to be or not.

Who would take care of Noah? I was strapped to a bed to avoid the onset of more contractions. I could kiss my own boo-boos.

Or not. I had to call my mother.

Here's the part of the story where my mother transforms from a shadowy figure on the sidelines to my hero. The one to whom I owe my life—twice. Wonder Mom. After this phone call, which I made from the deepest pit of despair I have ever sunken into, nothing would ever be the same between us. She said, "I'll catch a plane tomorrow morning."

She had a job that didn't offer any paid personal days. She didn't have money for a plane ticket. It never occurred to me that she could drop everything to pull me out of my pit. But maybe, I realized for the first time in my life, she hadn't rescued me before only because I had *never asked.*

Wasn't this a lesson I was learning again right now, on this trip to Michigan? That I have to *ask*? That if I want to connect with my family, I have to be willing to seek their help?

My doctor couldn't explain how I'd become pregnant on Depo Provera. "Ninety-nine percent is not the same as one hundred percent effective." I should have majored in statistics instead of English.

It was also possible, I later learned, that I had already been pregnant when I received my first Depo Provera shot, even though the test result at the doctor's office was negative. It was a urine test, and only a blood test can detect conception that has occurred within twenty-four hours. No one told me that, at the time. No one said the test might be false. All my doctor had said was that I was not and could not become pregnant.

But I did. My doctor explained the risks of a fetus on hormones. The baby could be a hermaphrodite. It could have major heart defects. If it were born extremely prematurely, which seemed likely given my shock-induced contractions, it might die at birth or suffer major brain damage. There were risks to my health too. Perhaps my life was not in danger, but it felt that way. I stared through the window at passersby on First Avenue and Sixteenth, walking in front of Beth Israel Hospital. I would have switched with any of them.

I had no choice but to give birth to a child whose life would be hell, whose father didn't want him, whose mother couldn't afford him. It was too late to have an abortion.

Or so I thought. It wasn't illegal to have an abortion after three months, but most doctors wouldn't perform one because they feared backlash from doctor-shooting protesters. "I know a guy," my doctor said. "He has a private clinic. All very hush-hush." He handed me the phone number on a sticky yellow square. "It's expensive," he said. "And obviously your insurance won't cover it."

My in-laws would help. Andrew had already asked them for money to cover the procedure, before he realized no doctor we knew would do it.

Only my husband, mother, and in-laws knew about my abortion. I told everyone else I had a miscarriage. My mother-in-law said, when she saw me next, "That's one way to lose weight fast." Then she added, "Thank God."

There was nothing I was more grateful for either, and yet I told almost no one. Not because of regrets. Not because I had a better choice. But because I didn't want to be judged. I didn't think I knew anyone else who'd had an abortion, which I know now wasn't true. Part of why women don't talk about their abortions is because women don't talk about their abortions. We're led to believe we're alone. If I wanted others to tell their stories, I should be willing to tell mine.

Barack Obama once said, "Those who diminish the moral elements of [abortion] aren't expressing the full reality of it," and I understand what he meant. I didn't want to punish myself, but I wanted to grieve. To mourn a loss, you have to first admit it exists.

You have acknowledged it. Talk about it. Wasn't that what I was learning on this trip too?

BACON CRUMBLED UNDER MY BUTTER knife. I opened my mouth, but the words would not come out. Not yet. So I remembered in silence, ladling runny yolk onto buttery pumpernickel toast.

After Barry paid the check, we left the moose heads behind and jumped back on I-75 North to exit 244. My brother, sister, and I used to count the exits all morning, eating Bugles and playing license plate games, when we made this trip as kids.

The trees hung heavy with snow, and the grass glazed with frost. Just a couple hundred miles from the city, we'd arrived in a colder, wilder place.

"You remember Dave Calkins?" Barry asked.

"Of course." We had talked about him the day before, about how he was with my father when he lost his hand.

"That's his house right there."

It was buried under a jungle of overgrown bramble and weeds. If I squinted, I could see in my mind's eye this scene:

I'm ten years old, with my grandmother and siblings. I can see her bringing Judy Calkins home-canned tomatoes and homemade jams.

The Calkins cabin, an unfinished skeleton of a house, has plastic flapping in the frames where the windows should be. A few interior walls separate the rooms, but no siding or clapboards seal the elements out. No electricity or running water, just an outhouse. Judy invites us in. There are so many kids I can't keep them straight or remember their names. In my hazy memory, there is a dog and a cat, and one of the youngest boys offers us a dog biscuit from a box. When we decline he says, "You like Cat Chow better?" and plucks kibble from the cat's bowl.

When my grandmother places some of her home-made Snickerdoodles on the diaper-covered coffee table, the children converge
like ants. I almost expect them to gobble me up too.

We children drive back to my grandparents' unfinished house
Up North, which seems, even without heat or electricity, like a pal-
ace now. "Those poor kids," my grandmother says, and in that word,
poor, I understand that wealth is relative. And so is luck. I breathe in
the scent left from my grandmother's cookies—cinnamon, butter,
and sugar.

BACK IN THE CAMRY, BARRY told me that Dave was my father's best
friend. I had no idea.

My memories of Dave don't include my father. I thought he was
just a family friend or second cousin or other relative. Now I wanted
to stop the car and run back to the house and knock on the door.
Besides my uncle and mother, Dave would be the person who best
knew my father. I should have been talking to him months ago. Years.

"Does he still live there?" I asked.

"Died a few weeks ago," Barry said. "We were up for the
funeral."

My body slumped into the seat. I was too late.

Barry described a man who looked like he was slow but was
actually a genius. I had never seen below the surface. He lived in
poverty, but he was smart enough, he could have made a fortune. As
his father had done before him, he spent a period working Downstate, sending money back to his family, but then he quit and moved
Up North, away from the pressures of urban living. "That kind of
boxed-in life was not for him."

Dave "taught himself to be an expert on every topic you could
think of," my uncle told me, but nobody saw how smart he was.
"He was one of those people who couldn't deal with social situa-
tions. He just lived in his own head."

For a while after high school, I learned, my father and Dave
lived together in an apartment in downtown Detroit, "virtually the

slums." When Barry moved in with them, they were living on caffeine and cigarettes and studying all kinds of religion and philosophy. "Fanatically."

They were starving themselves, living off God and air. Barry would buy five chicken pot pies for a dollar, cook them up, and make Dave and Jerry eat. They kept debating and reading, and finally Dave decided that the Seventh-day Adventists "were the way to heaven."

"Did my dad find his way?" I asked. Was he there now?

"He kept searching. Right up to when he died."

Jerry Lynn Calkins, the mentally challenged son Dave named after my father, was sent to a special school in Florida when we were children, and while living down there with his grandparents was sexually abused; in 1997 Jerry Lynn was himself convicted of child molestation. He's still in prison Up North. A few others had done jail time too.

These lost children, raised by the genius who was my father's soulmate, could have been me if my father had fallen that far off the grid. I could have lived their life, so far on the edge.

It was beginning to look like I wasn't a tragic children's book character just because my father died when I was young. In so many ways I was lucky.

ONCE WE ARRIVED AT THE house Up North, Barry took me for a walk.

It was hunting season for nothing, but pests don't count; you can shoot them any time. We were after porcupine. He fished out a pistol for me, but I didn't reach for it. "Not scared, are you?" He let out a gentle, affectionate laugh.

"No," I said, but my face doesn't lie. I'm sure he could see my eyes grow wide, my pale skin flush with blood.

As we hiked the land that had belonged in my family for generations, my body found its equilibrium. Something felt so familiar about the dirt under my feet.

Then I realized—it was flat. My soles understood how to grip the solid, midwestern plains. Out East, the ground slopes, forcing me to alternately push with my thighs or hit the brakes of my heels.

I bounded like a puppy. I scooped up snow and licked my hands. Connecting to this land was so simple.

We passed Sharon's Rock. I changed my mind; if I'm ever reincarnated, I don't want to come back as my daughter. Instead, I'd like to come back as myself on that rock.

We passed the apple tree my great-grandfather planted. My uncle's cousins wanted to hire a tree doctor to keep it alive. But Barry said sometimes you have to let things die. We reached the pipelines where we used to pick blackberries. The deer blind. The white pines. The red pines.

The snow whitewashed the ground. A blank white page. The air smelled like Christmas, evergreen everywhere, my own private North Pole, my life-sized snow globe.

Barry showed me where he had culled thousands of maple trees. He told me the animals were starting to come back.

So I was right. The forest of my childhood was barren. I'd always imagined an evil spell had cast the animals out, but now I asked him where they really went.

"Nothing for animals to eat out here," Barry explained. "The woods are dead."

Woods could die?

My grandfather couldn't bear to kill the trees my dad had planted. "I couldn't blame him," Barry said. "But that meant the whole damn forest went to hell." When trees get too crowded none of them can live. You have to clear space for the undergrowth to get sun.

We kept walking, past grove upon grove. "Maples are smart," Barry said. "They know when they have to stop growing or they'll die. Pine trees, like these, though, they're dumb. They'll keep growing even if it kills them. Which is what happened."

Sometimes things have to die so other things will live.

MONTHS EARLIER BARRY AND CORA had seen a large cougar a few miles from their house, and a ten-year-old girl had been attacked, not long before, by a bear. Barry brought the gun for more than porcupines.

If we didn't kill them first, he explained, they'd kill all the trees. The woods would go dead again. Porcupines used to have a purpose, thinning the forest, but they don't anymore. One porcupine will kill six trees. They girdle them, chew the bark off, and the tree dies. They don't have any predators. He laughed. "Except us."

We didn't shoot any porcupines that day, but my uncle told me more about the work he and my aunt have done to rejuvenate the forest. Culling trees and killing pests, then planting trees and growing plants for less harmful animals to eat. The woods depend on life and death, a balance of both, to thrive. Hunters could be conservators too, he explained, coaxing me to rethink my reflexive judgments against guns. Yet just looking at the cold metal caused me to bristle.

WE CLIMBED INTO THE DEER blind. "Now Jerry, he was a serious hunter," Barry said. "Me, I never cared if I killed anything or not. That's why Louis always wanted to go with me. Your dad was awfully hard on him."

"You knew?"

"All that corporal punishment got out of hand, I told Jerry that. But you couldn't win a fight with him."

I exhaled frost. It hung thick in the wind.

My grandpa couldn't win with my father either. He'd butt heads on purpose. The biggest thing they fought about? My dad "kept wrecking cars."

"You're kidding," I said.

"You didn't know that?"

The story I've always told myself is this: My father wasn't just a good driver, he was so good, he could work for the circus. He was a magician. He was Evil Knievel doing loop-de-loops on his motorcycle on television, but in a car.

"He was a *confident* driver," Barry said. "But that's not the same thing as *competent*."

Those qualities looked the same to my child eye.

"He would get so in depth into what he was thinking that he'd run red lights. He'd get into the kind of trance he had when he was reading a book. He couldn't hear or see what was in front of him."

He could have crashed while I was in the car. I was lucky to be alive.

Barry said, "What really twisted my dad up was what the insurance agent said. He wanted to cancel my dad's policy. And I'll never forget what he said that made my dad lose it. God's honest truth. I was standing right there. He said, 'Gerald will die in a car accident.'"

Barry paused. Put his gun down. Stopped looking up the trees. Then he actually chuckled. Something this dark is too hard to handle without a dose of humor. "Of course, he *did*."

BACK INSIDE, WE LUNCHED ON grilled cheese and tomato soup. We drank more coffee and leaned back in our stiff chairs. We ate cookies and licked the melted chocolate from our fingers. We untucked our shirts. Removed our shoes. And the layers that usually separate what we want to say and what we don't dare.

My sister. I needed to ask about Lynn.

Like Telemachus, looking for Odysseus, she made her father-finding trip at the age of twenty. Back then, my aunt and uncle owned a trailer down the road from our grandparents' house that they used as a base for winter sports during school vacations and any weekend they could spare eight hours for the round-trip drive. My siblings and I only came to the country in the summer. Our cousins could hotrod through the snow at the speed of fun. Lynn arrived one winter to join them.

AFTER BARRY'S RETELLING, I TOOK off on a hike by myself, playing back what he said, filling in details with my best guesses, trying to figure out what had gone through my sister's head. I imagined the visit like this.

LYNN STEERS HER BROWN FORD pickup north on I-75. She is the best driver in the whole family, even when she's just a few years past her high school road test.

Lynn looks like everything I want to be. A body made up almost entirely of long legs. (My legs are so short I have to special order long torso bathing suits and buy ankle length jeans.) Her mane of full, wavy, movie star hair rebukes my fine, limp strands.

She tunes the radio to Loretta Lynn, then AC/DC, a little bit coal miner's daughter, a little bit metalhead. She takes full command of the car, navigating without maps, swearing at the "sissy city" drivers holding back on the gas in the fast lane.

When she arrives at Barry and Cora's trailer, our cousins are huddled around a small table inside drinking hot chocolate after a morning of sledding at full-throttle speed. They're a few years younger than she is—seventeen, fifteen, and twelve.

With her cousins Lynn snowmobiles the afternoon away, gunning the pedal to the floor. Though she's never been on one before, she's always wanted to for as long as she can remember. It turns out she's a natural. Bundled up in so much down, she's impermeable. Even barreling into a mountain of snow won't hurt her. Nothing can.

She hauls the boys down a steep hill, she in her truck, they in their sleds. They luge, toboggan, slip and slide, skid and crash, topple and fly, over and over.

After dark, our cousins asleep in the bedroom at the back of the trailer, she stays till morning, sipping coffee with Barry and Cora. And venting. She asks Barry how our father died. And why. She asks about the dynamite and the FBI.

Barry answers then asks, "Why are you so mad?"

Lynn presses her fists into the table. "Isn't it obvious? If my dad hadn't been stupid enough to get himself killed, I wouldn't have had to wait till now to go snowmobiling for the first time."

"Hold on," Barry says. "You can say a lot of ill things about Jerry if you want. But my brother wasn't stupid."

"Stupid enough to not wear a seatbelt," she says.

"You're not being fair," Barry says. "Nobody wore them back then."

"I'm not being fair? Is this fair? We're all excited, we're going to drive Up North, and he can't get his lazy ass out of bed."

"But Lynn, are you aware of the fact that he worked all these jobs and whenever he had a day off he was dead on his feet?"

She is not.

"Go ask your Ma if you think I'm lying."

Lynn bites her lips. She is tough, even compared to the girls Barry has worked alongside on the pipelines in Alaska. She isn't the kind of girl who would cry in front of anyone. But the muscles in her face are stretched thin with the effort of holding it all in.

"I didn't know, all these years, you wanted to go snowmobiling so bad," he says.

She shakes her head. She can't speak or her mouth will fill with mucus. She shapes her hands like a container that fills up with the trailer, the land, the snow. Everything she wanted. All of *this*.

They sit in silence. Maybe they drink more coffee. No way they'll sleep now anyway.

"You know I hated you," she finally says.

Barry leans forward to hear. "Hated *who*?"

"You. For years and years."

"Because I didn't take you snowmobiling?"

"Because my daddy died and you got to live."

Barry gently taps her on the shoulder. Cajoling. "You don't feel that way now, do you?"

She exhales. "No."

I always knew my sister was angry, but I never knew why. She'd probably offer a different explanation now. She may not even know.

AFTER LUNCH, THE DIRT BECKONED again. I wound around the hundred forty acres. I followed every twist and turn of my sister's little kid logic till I realized I could no longer find my snowy trail. My feet should have known where to trample this familiar terrain, even if my brain was focused elsewhere. I was so tired and hungry even porcupine sounded good.

Then my aunt and uncle appeared like guardian angels, summoning me to dinner with my cousins up at the house.

"You weren't lost, were you?" they asked.

"Not anymore."

I RODE WITH MY AUNT and uncle through the Gum, the Dump, past stands of pine trees and maple. The open-topped Jeep rattled and bumped. Why did they have to drive a Jeep?

"You like hamburgers?" Cora asked me.

"Sure."

Barry tamped down the smile creeping up his face. "Maybe Sharon wants to shoot something for dinner instead."

"How can I, when you never taught me how?" I was teasing, just as he was. I'd never asked before, never wanted to learn. I thought it was clear, from the tightness of every muscle, from my shoulder to my temple, that I was gun shy, though I never knew exactly why.

But Barry said, "I can teach you now."

"Sure," I said, but my body said something else. I flinched, the way Noah did at first, when he started Little League, with James coaching his team. I ducked. I might have folded over if Barry hadn't noticed and said, "Maybe some other time."

The wind blew, and mounds of snow dropped from branches all around us. "Like I told Lynn about the snowmobiles, my folks wouldn't let me take you kids out to do nothing dangerous. Didn't want you running off in the woods with guns like Jerry and me did."

Something big rustled in a tree. We drove past too fast to see what it was.

"I don't want to rag on my folks. You've got to see it from their point of view," Barry said. "They lost everything when they lost Jerry. They couldn't stand to lose you too."

Barry's gun gleamed in the setting sun. Our orange caps matched the ball of orange setting low on the horizon, finally visible after we passed the multitude of thriving trees. I hugged my knees, so I wouldn't fall out, or maybe just because I wanted to hug something.

So I had lived my father's counter-life. My grandparents protected us, didn't allow us to stray into harm's way, because we were the legacy of their eldest child. We were like pheasants in a bird sanctuary. We lived the safe life my father didn't. Because he didn't.

THE TIRES CRUNCHED THE SNOW, covering the footprints I'd left in the path. On my hike, I'd wandered far astray. "I didn't know it then," Barry said, "but my folks did the right thing."

"What do you mean?" I asked.

"Look how you turned out," he said.

I flicked my palms toward my chin. "Me?" I couldn't even walk on a trail I'd tramped since I was practically born without getting lost.

"Yes, you," Cora said.

"I tell people," Barry said, "Google my niece, look at her education. Read all the stuff she writes. She's smart, just like her dad."

I stifled a few tears. I was about to have dinner with my cousins and didn't want them to see me look weak. Then I sat up straight against the hard back of my seat. I pulled my shoulders back and looked straight ahead.

I didn't think my family cared about what I wrote. My mother never read my poems or stories when I was young, though I'd craved her attention. Now I realize she simply hadn't had time.

My uncle pulled in next to the house. My muscles relaxed in a way they hadn't in years. Maybe ever. I stretched out my legs and allowed my body to take up as much space as I needed. This is what people must mean when they say, "Make yourself at home."

I did.

I was.

After all these years.

BY FIVE-THIRTY THE SKY blackened, except for the swath of stars shining like a ceiling of snow. After digging out the ice, Barry started a coal fire in the outdoor pit. Cora cooked the sides—steamed broccoli, canned baked beans, and a homemade apple pie she brought from her deep freezer Downstate.

My cousins helped retrieve chairs from the root cellar. I had been waiting to ask Barry about that time he took my mother out on a date. My mother had said I should. So I did.

"Date?" Barry repeated back to me.

"When Mom visited me in Paris she told me you once took her to a topless bar."

Barry laughed. "Oh yeah! I once took your ma to a titty bar, Starvin' Marvin's up on Fort Street. Ever been there? That place just closed down a couple months ago."

Too late again.

"Remember when we took your ma there?" Cora asked Barry.

"You took *Grandma?*"

"Actually, Barry's *dad* took us all," Cora said. "I wanted us all to go out to a nice dinner, which we did, and then Grandpa wanted to go to Starvin' Marvin's. I think your grandma was more at ease than I was."

Even in her wedding picture, when she was a nubile twenty-something, my grandmother looks matronly to me. I can't imagine anything more incongruous than her at a "titty bar."

Alma was a church-going lady who always wore a dress and lipstick, whose house and language was scrubbed clean, an upright woman who didn't truck with rowdy behavior. Even now it's hard for me to think of her as a sexual being. To see her comfortable at Starvin' Marvin's requires me to rethink everything I thought I knew about the place and about her.

I imagine my grandmother walking in the door. It's dimly lit but otherwise not much different than a diner. The hostess sports a short skirt that makes her look as if she's about to try a triple axel jump on the skating rink. Except if she did, her breasts, exposed and hanging freely, would hit her in the face and knock her down, they're so big and heavy.

The waitress ambles over matter-of-factly, pretending not to mind she's almost naked. Maybe she doesn't. My grandmother finds her nonchalance hilarious. She's in an alternate universe, one in which the bunnies in the Playboy calendars hung in the kitchen of the Kalkaska house have sprung to life. The waitress confirms their order, "Two bloodies and a screw," and my grandmother can't contain the giggles anymore. Everything's a *double-entendre*, and the waitress laughs along with her.

From what my mother had said in Paris, I'd assumed Barry was poking fun at her modesty, or sending a rebuke to my father for not taking my mother out himself. But Barry had just been trying to show her a good time at the local hangout. Stories change, of course, when different people tell them.

AFTER DINNER BARRY TOLD MORE childhood stories of making guns with my father and his cousins, then shooting them off in the basement of their house Downstate. Screwing odd parts together and constructing a makeshift cannon, with homemade gunpowder they'd baked on cookie sheets in the oven while their mother was at work. Driving over a hundred miles an hour more often than not, for hours at a time. Like everyone else in those days, without a seatbelt. Stories my cousins had heard over and over again. Each one of Barry's boys could have recited the stories about my father to me, with all the embellishments Barry has added over the years.

I wanted to enclose myself in the shelter of those stories, the ones I was hearing for the first time. I wanted their familiarity, through repetition, to come to seem the same as their truth.

WHEN WE FINALLY DROVE BACK Downstate, we took the same road my father and sister had traveled on the night of the fatal crash. Barry pointed out the place where they'd been found. It felt like a pilgrimage site, a sacred spot. I almost expected something supernatural to happen. I hadn't forgotten my premonition.

This was where my father's body was found, sprawled on the road, with Lynn still inside the Jeep.

"The Jeep was hardly hurt," Barry said.

"But it was totaled," I said.

"They always total a vehicle when there's a death. And my dad said, 'I'm going to buy that jeep.' I told him, 'Don't you *ever* bring that Jeep around me. Because that *damned* Jeep killed my brother.'"

"The Jeep? Why the Jeep?"

"You don't know the whole story?"

He didn't even wait for me to say it. That I didn't know shit.

"The cops said he fell asleep," Barry said.

"But he couldn't have fallen asleep," Cora said. "He'd just bought gas. He had the receipt in his shirt pocket."

So why did the cops lie? Were they lazy or corrupt?

"He hadn't driven but a few miles," Barry started.

"And then he hit a deer," I said. That part I knew.

"No," Barry said.

"He didn't hit a deer?"

Barry said, "This is what the skid marks say. He hit the brakes and slid. He turned this way, went so many feet, hit the brakes and slid, and when he cut back, he rolled. There were deer tracks in the area. Your ma told me Lynn saw a deer footprint. Lynn said they were hit by a deer. But that's probably just a child's vision."

"Lynn was sleeping," Cora said.

"But she woke up and saw a deer," I said. "She drew a picture of a deer. A picture of her and the deer and the Jeep."

"She was just a tiny kid," Barry said.

She was also the only living witness.

"There's two exits at Harrison," Barry said. "At the first exit, Jerry stopped at the gas station, then he got back on the highway. At the second exit, there was a bar on this side of the interstate." He pointed. "A buddy of mine who lives in Harrison told me it's real common for drunks to come out of that bar heading the wrong way on the interstate. The skid marks look like this—hit your brakes, swerve, hit your brakes, swerve. Like Jerry was *dodging* another vehicle."

Cora said, "But a deer doesn't dart back and forth."

"What's the death certificate say?" I asked.

"That he fell asleep," Barry said.

"Nobody ever told me he fell asleep."

"I'm telling you he didn't," Barry said. "They put that down because the Jeep wasn't hurt. He might have *dodged* a deer. Might have. But the skid marks look more like he dodged a car. It was dark and foggy. About two in the morning. I can see the skid marks to this day. I can see where he slid. And when he cut it back he rolled. Had he had a seatbelt on he wouldn't have died. He probably would not have been even hurt."

"He might have broke an arm or something," Cora said.

This is the part that really makes me want to go back in time. This is the thing I most want to fix. All I want to do is slip the metal in the slot. All I want to do is strap him in.

"Why'd the Jeep tip?" I've swerved before but never toppled over.

"Those old CJ5 Jeeps were squirrely," Barry said. "I drove it through Detroit after he first got it. A car cut me off, and I cut it and it felt like it went up on two wheels and we both said, 'Oh God!'"

I let out a puff of air.

"The old CJ5s had a high center of gravity. The more modern CJ5s have four-wheel independent suspension—that's what the army had when I was in there. And they squat. You can't hardly make 'em flip. But a civilian CJ5, they flip."

"That seems like a major design flaw," I said.

"Like I told my dad," Barry said, "That damn Jeep killed my brother."

Not a deer. Though my sister might still say it was.

According to my uncle, all my life I had been telling myself the story of my father's death *all wrong*.

IF I KNEW ONE THING, I thought it was about the deer. *He went hunting for a deer and the deer killed him.* No and no. Neither happened.

It was too early in November for deer season, and they'd gone hunting for small game. The buck with mammoth antlers that knocked over the Jeep was a myth. A monster. A vegetarian Godzilla. A Bigfoot Bambi. The meat that meted out its own punishment. The revenge of the prey no longer makes any sense.

WE PULLED INTO MY AUNT and uncle's driveway in Carleton and took a walk around their property to stretch our legs from the long drive. The snow Downstate was wimpier than in the country.

"Not all your stories are the same as my mom's," I said.

He let out a long, slow breath. Finally, he said, "Make no mistake, my brother was no saint. He hit your ma."

"You knew?"

"Didn't mean I could stop it."

We trudged along, our boots slushing the white fluff.

"I told him it wasn't right. He was tough on your brother too."

The sun sat on the horizon.

"There's a lot of things Jerry shouldn't have done. As I'm sure you know."

I was trying to remember.

"It's God's truth, Jerry was flawed," Barry said. "I couldn't say that, though, while my dad was alive."

"Why not?"

"You ever hear the phrase 'Death cleanses'? What that means is that after somebody dies nobody says anything bad about them. They become saints. That's what my folks did with Jerry."

Death cleanses our memory. It can whitewash the stories we tell. Brainwash us into thinking we're grieving over someone who is more than human.

Look at the euphemisms in the obituary section of my local paper. When someone dies, he "joins the angels," "is called to the Lord," "climbs the stairway to heaven," "gets his wings," "joins the heavenly choir," or "returns to the mind of God."

BARRY SAID, "MY FOLKS FOUGHT with Jerry tooth and nail when he was alive, but they forgot all that after he died."

Just as I, as a child, forgot most of the bad things. And my brother forgot most of the good things. Death sometimes erases our hard drives, like a computer virus. Or maybe it just shakes things up a bit, like a snow globe.

"After he died, my folks thought Jerry had done no wrong," Barry said. "And I had done nothing right." Funny how malleable memory can be.

Barry continued, "I always said, 'Dad, you just don't remember right.' 'Your ass,' he'd say, 'I know exactly right.' And, you know, I would have had to study chemistry and have one hand and not have gone to Vietnam for all his facts to be correct, but he wouldn't back down from his version of the truth." Don't we all have a different version?

Barry and my grandpa argued about my father. Frequently. But he wouldn't hear Barry, even though he was right in front of him.

"Right up until my dad died," Barry said, "Anything that was wrong, when we were kids, I did it. Anything that was right, that was thanks to Jerry, in his book."

It was all—finally—starting to make sense.

"I loved Jerry," he said. "My brother was my best friend. I took his death real hard. I was so depressed, for months I couldn't even work. But I didn't love him so much that I forgot who he was. I think I got over his death enough to see him as a real person. My ma and dad, they never did. For the rest of their lives, they made Jerry into a god."

The stories my grandparents told me romanticized my father into a god too. Now I knew where the legends of my super-father came from. It's hard to feel close to a god. At last, with what I knew now, my father seemed to be right next to me.

And then he was gone.

"Right before I was drafted, me and him were working three jobs," Barry said. "Jerry did that more than me. He would go from one job to the next to the next to the next."

How could anyone work three jobs? When I worked one and a half, a full-time job and a part-time one, I had barely enough energy to think.

Barry and my father were Up North one day. One fall afternoon in 1974. The woods were alive, animals everywhere. The brothers were walking down Campbell Road, and my father said, "What I wouldn't give to be laid off right now, coming into small game season.'"

Rabbits and pheasants, the kind of hunting my father lived for.

"You need to get a pipeline book," Barry told him. "Seems like I'm laid off more than I work."

My father said, "My Pontiac's paid for, my Jeep's paid for, my house is paid for, and I got ten grand in the bank. So I'm going to cut back on some of these extra jobs and start to enjoy life a little bit."

Then two weeks later he was dead.

At thirty-two, he was on the brink of a new life, about to start over. He'd been working more than one job, dog tired from the strain of being the sole financial support of his family and struggling with a less-than-satisfying marriage.

Sound familiar?

At thirty-two, I was working two jobs, freelance at home, full time during the day, socking every penny away to allow me to leave an unhappy marriage. That whole year I was keenly aware of my mortality. I wasn't sure I deserved to live to thirty-three.

Because he didn't.

But I did. At thirty-three, I finally started to "enjoy life a little bit." Or, actually, a lot. The best things in my life happened after thirty-three. Everything turned around for me then. The year I met James.

What might have changed for my father if he had been able to turn thirty-three? So many possibilities. Love, peace, joy? I'll never know.

Because my father died before he'd really *lived*.

But here I was, living still. Wasn't investigating my father's life supposed to kill me?

There was one thing I hadn't yet asked. Maybe that would do it.

"Why does our family hate the cops? Because of how the FBI treated you and Dave at the hospital?"

"You don't know the story about the cops? You're shitting me, Sharon."

"I don't know anything." Let that be my default answer to everything. Put it on repeat.

"I'm sure you heard it as a kid. Numerous times."

What could I say? I've blocked these memories out? Not that I meant to, I just did? I'm not stupid, just naïve? Like a woman? No. I shrugged. So he told me.

When my father was killed he was lying in the middle of the road. In the Jeep he had a 25/20, a collector's gun that belonged to my grandpa, and he had a custom made, left-handed, three-inch magnum shotgun. Both valuable objects. When Barry and my grandpa picked up his personal possessions, those guns were gone. When they asked the cops for the guns, they said there were no guns. That somebody must have stolen them.

At Hydromation Engineering, Barry worked with a Wayne

County sheriff. They became friends. He figured that Harrison police department, "little hick-town cops," stole the guns.

The only money the police handed over to them was a little change from my father's shirt pocket, with a receipt. He had just bought gas and something for my sister to eat, at a gas station one exit before the place where he was killed.

I could taste the food my father used to buy me on those trips Up North. My favorite meal was a hot roast beef sandwich, open faced, with mashed potatoes and gravy. He'd insert a few coins into a vending machine, then place the plate in the gas station micro-wave. It was probably filled with every preservative in the dictionary, but to me it was the definition of delicious.

My father had just cashed his paycheck, hundreds of dollars, enough money to pay a dentist he owed. But his wallet was missing. That money was all gone.

"This is why your grandpa hated the cops so bad," Barry said, "and it didn't do me no good either when it comes down to it. I knew something smelled bad, so I got hold of my buddy and he said, 'There's nothing I can do but I can stir the water a little bit and they can think I'm doing something.' Miraculously enough," Barry said, sarcastically, "the Harrison police found Jerry's guns right after that. Of course the money was still gone."

Barry's speech quickened, his voice rose. He's not the kind of man who angers easily, not like my father. He's the reasonable one, the straight man, the mediator who always counseled his brother to try harder to keep the peace. But listening to him now, as he continued the story, I could imagine his cursing then, at those greedy thieves.

Barry and my grandpa drove up to the Harrison police department. The cop told them my father's wallet was lying in the middle of the road when they initially picked up his belongings weeks before. The police pulled my father's file and they showed them some "extremely graphic" pictures. My father had his hand up and he was totally covered in blood, but his wallet was visible in his back pocket.

"The lying bastard was right across the room," Barry said. "And I said to the cop that was showing me these pictures, the same one we talked to right after the accident, 'What is that right there?' I put my finger on what would be his wallet in his back pocket. The cop's exact words were 'Anybody can see that's his wallet.' Then I ran my mouth off with every swear word I could think of and said, 'That's exactly right and that lying bastard told me my brother's wallet was laying in the road. Then I turned and said, 'You stole Jerry's money and his guns.'"

"That's disgusting," I said. The Kentucky Fried Chicken we'd eaten on the way home threatened to gurgle up in my throat.

"Wait, it gets worse," Barry said. "My dad really twisted. We caused such a ruckus in there they *physically* threw us out of that police station with Jerry's guns and told us if we ever set foot back in, if any word ever got back that we'd returned to town, if they ever got a whiff we were asking anything about what happened to Jerry's body or Jerry's belongings or Jerry's anything, they'd make sure we never got out of Harrison *alive*."

I was shivering, and not because my boots were soaked with grassy snow.

That's why I'd been so sure that asking about my father might kill me. Because the Harrison police had said so.

And the guns. Did this story explain my fear of firearms? My instinct to stay away from them?

Barry said, "I'm amazed you didn't know it. Louis said he hadn't heard it either, when I saw him at Thanksgiving."

My brother heard this story before I did too. Lynn, twenty years ago. Louis, last year. What took me so long?

But I had to admit there was something familiar about the tale too. I could feel the cadences of all those curses running through my blood. I didn't consciously remember, but now the words were flooding back. I'm sure I overheard my uncle and grandfather ranting about the police. I must have known about the threat and suppressed the memory. I thought the police might kill my uncle and my grandfather, that all my family's men would die.

That I might die too. That was where my premonition came from—the Harrison police. This was the answer I'd come all this way for. As a child, interpreting grown-up's words in a literal way, the risk had seemed real. My dread had stayed with me till now, when I finally understood how ridiculous it was.

It was time to go in. We shook our snowy boots on the porch, then opened the door.

WE STAYED UP LATE ON the last night of my trip. I was acutely aware of my time running out.

We carried up from the basement boxes of photographs my grandmother had accumulated over her lifetime. I'd never seen so many pictures of my father. I didn't know so many existed. School pictures in stiff ties. Pictures from the state fair. Huckleberry picking. Hunting and fishing. The green Jeep he died in, that detestable vehicle. A photo of my mother inscribed to my grandmother, "You are like a mother to me. You are kindness itself. That is why I am going to name my first daughter after you." Another name I was not given. Alma means *soul* in Spanish. I like to think I've inherited part of Alma's soul—the practical, cheerful, hardworking part. "I was almost named after Grandma," I said.

"She was the rock of the family," Barry said. "No question. Dad fell apart when Jerry died. But Ma, you could just see her stop herself from crying, pull herself together, and do what had to be done." I was lucky to have such an unbreakable woman as a role model.

"Maybe we can find the guest book from the funeral in one of these boxes," Cora said. I'd told her how much my mother wished she had it. How much I did too.

We couldn't find that book, but we found another belonging to my father, the only one I've ever seen, which seems strange, given what a famously voracious reader he was. Cora asked if I wanted to take it home.

Of course.

Then she handed me Homer's *Odyssey.* I couldn't believe it. This was like an omen from the gods.

I FEEL AS IF I'VE been reading *The Odyssey* my whole life. My father must have read it to me, from this very copy.

It seems fitting that on this trip my aunt and uncle gave me this book, with my father's name inscribed and notes peppered throughout. It's the only book of his I own. A treasure. A relic even. I will listen to it, as quietly and purposefully as a hunter listens as she waits for a porcupine to pop its head out of a hole in a tree before shooting.

This is one thing the book says to me: Odysseus took decades to return to Ithaca from Troy. He was sidetracked and detoured, sirened and lured, tempted and tricked. Yet he never gave up hope. He finally made it home. So have I.

Part 7
Phantom Limbs

Overleaf: My siblings and me with my father's six-point buck, 1970

November 2013 and beyond

I STILL LIVE IN A college town. I'm still married to a professor. Most of my friends are still academics and other brainy types. But I'm not *pretending* I'm one of them anymore. I *am*. Who says I can't be?

I've earned my place, but I was born into it too. My father finished only one year of college, but he was a self-educated polymath. The two of us have more in common than I ever knew. He crashed cars and hit his wife, but he bore within himself scars that I can only guess at, scars like the ones on the knoblike stump where his right hand used to be. Until it wasn't.

The story I used to tell about myself was this: I'm a phony. Maybe we all are. How often is the way we see ourselves different from how the world perceives us?

And it's not as if "the world" has one set of eyes. Who we are depends on who you ask. If I learned anything from my search for my father, it's this: We all are moving targets.

Or maybe our portraits are more like mosaics assembled from shards of pottery to compose a face, each shard representing a story one person tells about us. When I asked my mother about my father, she gave me a few flecks of ceramic. I connected them and thought that, together, they made his portrait. But she only knew the part of him that was her husband. He wasn't sexist, she said. He wasn't a monster. He was just a man.

According to my brother, our father was a bully. My sister mostly remembered him as the man who died instead of her, the man whose death made her feel guilty for living.

From Barry, I heard the story of my father as a son and a brother, his best friend and the smartest kid in the whole school. What would Dave Calkins have added to the mosaic of my father, the companion of his monk-like studies in that narrow Cass Corridor apartment? If I had caught Dave just weeks earlier, when he was still alive, I might have had to tilt my father's portrait to the right or left or even hang it upside-down.

Had I been able to talk to my grandparents, would they have changed the story they told me all my life, that their son could do no wrong? Maybe they would have told me how much of him they saw in me.

After all, we both liked to take risks. We were brave or reckless—or both.

I finally realized what playing with dynamite meant. Digging up the past, exposing family secrets to the world. Writing this book.

Joan Didion also famously said that writing is a hostile act, that we're always selling people out. What happens when they discover that?

When I returned to Virginia, my father's copy of *The Odyssey* in my bag, I decided to carry more of him back than just that book. I took his chutzpah. I took his nerve. I took, if not his actual self-confidence, his talent for pretending.

I e-mailed my friend Rachel, director of the local nonprofit literary center, and told her I'd like to teach creative writing classes. I had an MFA, and I'd published four dozen essays and short stories—more than most other writing instructors there. I'd always wanted to teach, and the only thing preventing me was my conviction that I didn't deserve to.

Rachel and I met for lunch at a local Indian restaurant. I brought a file full of paperwork, expecting to have to win her over, to prove my credentials. Instead, she just said, "Fiction or nonfiction?"

"Either," I said. Could it be that easy?

"We have the biggest need in memoir," she said. "We've never done a book-length course. Or a year-long one. Think you could create a few?"

When my first boss sat me down in his office and told me I needed assertiveness training, I'd never followed his advice. Or maybe I had. Perhaps my search for my father was really a crash course in how to assert myself.

I could feel my father's red hair shine in me, his fierce opinions, his unrelenting drive. I found the smart aleck and the show off. I found him and I kept him. I let him say, in my voice, "Of course I can. When do I start?"

MEANWHILE, ANDREW E-MAILED ME AGAIN, complaining that Noah wouldn't answer his messages or calls.

"He keeps asking me to visit for Christmas," Noah explained. "And I can't. We're too alike." I knew what he meant: Noah was starting to acknowledge his own anxiety. His father had panic disorder and agoraphobia, which kept him from working and driving and even doing simple things like meeting a friend for lunch. Noah needed a little distance from his paternal genes. He needed time to figure out the ways in which he was alike and different from his father. He needed to do a compare and contrast, as I had just done with mine.

Noah took the semester off, and his anxiety was finally formally diagnosed and treated, with medication and meditation. He started talking to his father again, now that he was no longer afraid of becoming him. Then Noah decided to make a clean break and switch schools. He applied to five competitive colleges and was accepted into every one.

I TAUGHT CITY PLANNERS, SCIENTISTS, professors, teachers, counselors, and a psychologist who'd published half a dozen self-help books. During my first class, half my students wanted to hire me to edit their whole books. Jackie, one of my students, was writing a book about lost connections. She grew up in a small town, attending the same school as her cousins, whom she was not allowed to acknowledge, even when she saw them in the halls or auditorium. Her father cut off his brother, and her mother cut off her sister. After both parents died, Jackie decided to connect, for the first time, with her aunts and uncles and cousins, people she'd heard were evil. Of course, she discovered they weren't.

Jackie had grown up surrounded by these people, whom she had never talked to before. They were both there and not, their absence making them even more present. Like my sister. Like so many people who told me their stories of lost family connections as soon as I told them my own.

"What should I call my book?" Jackie asked.

I said, "How about *Phantom Limbs?*"

"AFTER ONE OF YOUR LIMBS is amputated, you may feel as if the limb is still there," according to the National Institutes of Health. I wonder if my father felt his missing hand, when he was alive. I wonder if he can tell that I still feel him, even after he's gone. "This is called phantom sensation," NIH tells me. The part that has been severed may seem "tingly, prickly, numb." That's how I felt as a child. Numb. "Hot or cold." Sometimes I have felt both, at the same time, for my father. "Like your missing toes or fingers are moving." Just because something is absent doesn't mean it's static. "These sensations slowly get weaker and weaker," the helpful medical web site says. "You should also feel them less often." But, of course, "they may never go away completely."

I WON PRIZES, LIKE THE one that sent me to Key West to give a reading. My students and clients snagged agents and book deals. They published in national newspapers and magazines. I put on dresses and heels for class, trying to impersonate a teacher. An expert. Someone who knew what she was talking about. Then finally I realized that's what I had become.

The next October, a year after Bob died, James's mother, two brothers, and his sister flew to California to spread Bob's ashes in the Sierra Nevada, where he took week-long hiking treks for decades.

I called my mother to confirm her plans to visit me over Halloween, as she did every year. "I meant to tell you," she said. "Joe and I were in an accident." Again, I found out only after calling about something else.

They were driving back from lunch when Joe veered off the highway and passed out. Luckily they swerved into a grassy median, not another car, not a deer, not a precipice, nor an eighteen wheeler full of oil. They weren't hurt, but Joe's doctors wouldn't allow him to drive again until a pacemaker stopped making his heart skip beats. My mother was shaken up but unhurt.

She arrived in Virginia, and we watched *Secondhand Lions,* my Aunt Gail's favorite movie. "She watched this over and over again, in hospice," my mother said. I almost felt as if I'd been there with Gail, as she slipped away. I almost forgave my mother for not telling me Gail was sick until she was already gone. Then I did forgive. Of course I did.

I took my mother and Ella to Fashion Square Mall to buy school clothes. We baked oatmeal cookies, listened to Ella play cello, and hiked Crabtree Falls, our dog bounding ahead and my mother scampering to keep up. She practiced flute every day, showed me her favorite paintings on the Metropolitan Museum app she'd downloaded on her tablet, and traded baseball statistics with James.

"Roast potatoes or mashed" I asked her one evening as I started dinner.

"Whatever's easiest," she said, as usual.

In the past, I would have said the same thing when asked. About anything. But now I wanted an opinion, the stronger the better. "You have to pick one," I said. And she finally did.

The most remarkable thing about the visit was how unremark-able it was. I had braced myself for more revelations about my father, but for the first time in recent years, she offered me none. Maybe she had already shared them all.

THEN, FOR CHRISTMAS, JAMES, NOAH, Ella, and I traveled to Aus-tin to visit my brother and his wife Janet, another Renaissance art historian, opera buff, and absurdly elegant dresser. We walked into their living room, lined with old Victrolas Lou had bought from estate sales and was in the process of restoring. He pointed to a box with a ribbon around it and said, "This one's for you." We unbuck-led the case and he played us a 78 of the Harrigan song on the 1929 Columbia Model 202, a portable machine "suitable for taking on picnics," the user's manual said.

"Can I crank it?" Noah asked. "How does it work?" For the whole trip, Noah glued himself to Lou, listening to every word.

Noah pulled a ukulele from his bag, and Louis responded by showing him YouTube videos of his favorite ukulele players, includ-ing a clip of Kate Micucci playing "Dear Deer," which begins like this.

> Dear deer
> I am writing you a letter
> In the hopes that you'll know better
> Not to go in the woods in Pennsylvania
> 'Cause my dad's in a tree waiting to kill ya
> Just be warned.

"Story of my life," Lou said.

I settled into the Craftsman settee and scanned his shelves. Manga, graphic memoir, art history books that weigh a hundred pounds. Photos of Arts and Crafts bathrooms, Japanese dictionaries, and flash cards.

Louis pulled a couple yellowed textbooks off his shelf. "These are the ones Dad used to teach me German," he said. "Look at his handwriting. Doesn't look as masculine as you'd think, does it?"

I showed Lou my photo album, the one our grandmother had given me as a present for my high school graduation. "This is one of my favorites," I said, pointing to a picture of us three kids in front of my grandparents' red Pontiac, draped with a freshly killed deer. My grandmother's caption says it's a six-point deer my father killed. In the picture, Louis strokes the animal's muzzle with one hand, his other hand stashed in his pocket, and his face twisted into a grimace. On his left, I pet the buck's hoof. Lynn stands between us.

"I look pretty dubious about the whole thing," Lou said. "But you seem to be having a good time."

"We had to get used to touching dead things," I said.

"Yeah. This picture reminds me of a couple years later when Dad was in his coffin and Grandma insisted that I touch him. For some reason, I wouldn't. She insisted and insisted, and I kept refusing. I never did—it just seemed pointless to touch a man I never touched while he was alive."

AT A KOREAN BBQ THAT evening, the server said to my brother, "You're a doctor!" At first I had no idea she was calling him a "Dr. Who."

"People tell me that all the time," Lou said. "You know, the bow tie, the glasses."

She hovered at our table, recounting with my brother, episode after episode of the TV show, comparing various incarnations and actors. I watched Noah's eyes widen as he witnessed his uncle's encyclopedic recall. I'd grown up with Louis's memory magic tricks, but I tried to see him fresh through my son's eyes.

For our trip's grand finale, we drove outside the city limits for authentic, downhome BBQ. We parked in a Texas-sized lot and ordered ribs and brisket by the pound and beans and cole slaw, then scooped it all out onto wax paper on picnic tables, because this was the kind of restaurant where plates were for sissies. The kind of place where my father would have felt right at home.

Noah asked Lou, "Did you ever watch *Mork and Mindy?*" Robin Williams, one of Noah's heroes, had recently died, and *Mork and Mindy* was his breakout hit.

Williams always reminded me of my brother. Louis isn't a comic, but he's a performer, always gesturing in large, enthusiastic sweeps, with the same manic energy. On past trips when I'd sat in on one of Louis' classes, the way he stood on the table and belted out quotes made me think of Williams in *Dead Poets Society.*

"One of my favorite shows," Louis said.

"What else did you watch as a kid?" Noah asked. "My mom says *The Incredible Hulk* and *Planet of the Apes* scared her to death."

"If you want to talk TV, ask my sister Lynn," Louis said. "She watched it nonstop." Then he proceeded to name her shows: *Dallas* and *Love Boat* and *Fantasy Island* and more I can't even remember. He recounted the plots, in detail, of several episodes, naming the characters and the actors who played them.

"You didn't watch those shows?" Noah asked. "Sounds like you did."

"They were just on," Louis said. "I heard the noise through the thin walls."

Here my brother was doing magic again. All he had was background noise seeping through the plaster separating the living room from his bedroom, but even then, even when he wasn't actively paying attention (when he was, in fact, trying hard to block the sounds out so he could read *Thus Spake Zarathustra* or *Dr. Faustus* or whatever his thick library book of the week was) his photographic memory was taking snapshots that he could still recall, decades after, and offer Noah. And yet Lou still didn't remember what he didn't want to.

Later, in the car, I told Noah, "I barely remember those shows."

He tried to console me. "It's genetic." (But there's no one I share more genes with than my brother.) "You're born with that kind of memory or you're not." And then all I heard were Noah's gulps for breath.

"Are you OK?" I asked, from the front seat.

"I miss him," Noah said. "I miss Uncle Lou."

"I know."

I had cried too, after I said good-bye to my uncle. On my solo trip back from Michigan, after interviewing Barry and Cora, I sat on the plane, buckled up, closed my eyes, and let the tears fall. I wasn't just crying then because I missed my uncle, but because I missed my father. I missed him in a way I couldn't have missed him before, because now he was real.

I'd clutched the photos of my father's childhood that Cora retrieved for me from boxes in her basement. I'd palmed my phone, containing my uncle's interviews, hours and hours describing years and years. I was taking home so much more than I came with.

But also so much less. I left behind my insecurity. I'd had that burned out of me on that journey, just as my uncle said Vietnam had burned the insecurity out of him.

Mostly I'd cried on the plane for the years of lost connection. The years I'd stayed away. Maybe the whole point of my quest had been to reconnect with my aunt and uncle and cousins—my family—again.

In our rental car in Austin, Noah slowed his breathing enough to say, "Can we come back here next Christmas too? Next time, let's not stay away so long."

I WENT TO THE GYM one day, as always, with my phone. I don't like to exercise without a soundtrack. This time, when I put my music on Shuffle, I didn't hear Beyoncé, Talking Heads, or The Killers. I heard myself. I was asking questions about my father on my recording app, interviewing my aunt and uncle. My voice sounded too squeaky, too hesitant and breathy to accompany the pounding of feet on the treadmill.

I'd recorded almost ten hours of material on my research trip to Michigan. I'd copied the audio files onto my computer, transcribed them, and turned them into stories. But I also apparently left them on my phone.

I must have meant to carry around these voices, telling me about my father's life and death. I wanted to carry him with me. Always.

No other object was so valuable that I felt compelled to keep it on my person all through the day. In my pocket, in my purse, in my hand. Always charged, always consulted.

The back was cracked, but I didn't fix it. Maybe I liked it that way. Cracked like my voice, straining to ask what I'd never dared before. Cracked like a fissure, between Before and After.

WHAT WOULD MY FATHER HAVE thought of my book and the journey I took to write it? I want to think he would be proud of me.

What would he have made of the event that started it all—Ella's eighth birthday party, where the boys waged war with rubber duckies and the girls staged a protest, raising balloons in the air and marching across the lawn, shouting, "We want peace! We want peace!"

I'm glad my father was a radical. He gave me a copy of Thoreau's *Walden* and Salinger's *The Catcher in the Rye* as soon as I could read. He told me real life exists only off the grid, though I had no idea what that meant. He said, "Don't forget that grown-ups are phonies."

I like to think if my father were alive today, he would teach Ella how to weld with one hand, how to drive with no hands, how to kill and skin and clean wild animals and eat off the land. He would have become more patient and calm, less angry and violent. He would have become as different from his younger self as I am from mine, if only he hadn't run out of time.

What would my father call my brother if he saw him today—an art history professor who favors tweed and bowties, an opera fan who decorates his house with antiques? If he saw my sister—living in the woods with bison and mountain lions, renovating houses, and chopping wood? Would he laugh at the way I spend my life behind a desk, or would he smile and ask, "What are you trying to do, write the next *Catcher in the Rye?*"

If he saw my mother—learning to play a musical instrument for the first time in her sixties and traveling to Italy and eating whatever she wants, would he recognize the docile girl barely out of her teens who knew she had to put dinner on the table with freshly squeezed lemonade the precise moment he walked in the door?

If he had the chance, my father might have grown as much as my mother has. If he had lived to be as old as I am now, he might have experienced a grand epiphany, like a character in a novel. More likely, he would have changed with the times, as so many others did, embracing his more feminine side once it became more socially acceptable to do so.

At our local elementary school, even the boys are required to take dance classes, and the high school has an active LGBTQ club, with a legion of straight supporters. My adolescent daughter counts among her friends half a dozen trans or gender fluid kids. My father could have embraced these changes. He may have welcomed the chance to redefine masculinity as something other than control. He was, after all, a man who knew how to adapt, turning his one-handedness into an opportunity for performance. "Look," he seemed to say when he drove, "I don't even need the one I have."

He might have shared Noah's passion for old spaghetti Westerns. They'd watch *Django*, the 1966 Italian film. When the bad guys think our hero's dead but he lifts his head and pulls the trigger with his mouth, my father might have said, "I could do that, too."

He could teach my son and daughter to make peace without being phonies. He could tell them to be proud of me, their mother, for becoming a writer and teacher. Because he died so young, I can fill in his future myself.

ONE MORNING THAT WINTER, I opened the side door to let my dog out, and she disappeared in the mist. The yard was covered with the kind of fog that could hide ghosts.

I don't really believe in ghosts, but there is something about water-saturated air that's almost supernatural, something that reminds me of my father, probably because he permanently disappeared into fog.

When I drove to class, the fog still clung. Jennie, one of my students, is a meteorologist, so we often talk about the weather. I told her that the night my father died was foggy like this, that I'd always wondered exactly what he saw out his windshield and if he would have died had the sky shown clear.

"You can find out," she said.

"I can?"

She told me about a database, started by her PhD advisor and one of her fellow students at the University of Michigan. It retrieves archived information about historical weather, hour by hour. We brought up the site and typed in the date and place where my father took his last road trip.

"THE FOG WAS REALLY THICK," Jennie said. No wonder my mother had begged him to postpone. Visibility ranged from 0.5 to 0.1 miles ahead, with 93 percent humidity. The wind was strong, blowing in from the north, pushing smoke into the fog.

"Visibility that poor is rare," Jennie said. "For a lot of his trip, it was 0.1 miles. That's the lowest the database can record. It could have been virtually zero."

"So he was driving blind?" I asked.

"Looks like it."

I pointed to one of the columns. "What does smoke mean?"

"Probably industrial from the factories. We're talking about Detroit. Before the Clean Air Act. But it's extremely rare for smoke to be so thick it shows up as weather."

Even if I'd sat in the passenger seat of the Jeep with my father, even if I'd been standing along the road or filming him from above, I may never have known whether he fell asleep or his Jeep hit another car or a deer. My sister probably didn't really see, either, though she drew a deer in her picture version of the accident. Some things will always remain hidden, no matter how hard we search for them.

According to another site Jennie pulled up for me, fog is composed of the same water droplets that make up clouds. The only difference is that clouds stay in the sky and fog hovers close to the ground.

I can't be sure I've discovered the whole truth of my father's story or even of my own—if such truth is even possible given the haze inherent in memory. Perhaps he lingers in the clouds, maybe not the ones that make it all the way up to heaven, but the ones that can't quite leave the earth.

I like to imagine my father is still floating in that fog. I like to imagine I'm not anymore. After all, I can imagine whatever I want.

Acknowledgments

Some of the sections in this book were published in previous form in *The New York Times* (Modern Love) and *The Rumpus*. I am grateful to their editors, Daniel Jones, Samantha Riley, and Arielle Bernstein, for recognizing the potential in this material and helping me polish it. I would also like to thank Allison Wright (*Virginia Quarterly Review*), Jane Lancellotti (*Narrative*), and Brad Listi (*The Nervous Breakdown*), who edited and published other essays and encouraged me to write about some of the topics I cover in this book.

I would like to thank the Virginia Center for the Creative Arts, where parts of this book were written, and the BAMA Works Fund of the Dave Matthews Band, which supported my stays there.

My wonderful agent, Gail Hochman—warm, insightful, and wise—has been my guide and unfailing champion throughout the writing of this book.

To my editor, Barbara Smith Mandell: Thank you for believing in this book from the beginning and for sending the manuscript to the anonymous peer reviewers who so deeply understood my story and the unusual technique I use to tell it. Thank you to the team at Truman State University Press: Lisa Ahrens, for her beautiful design; Jacob Condon, for his marketing savvy; and Monica Barron, editor of the Creative Nonfiction series, for her vision. I am also grateful to the Mindbuck Media team, Jessica Glenn and Rebecca Kelley, for their publicity expertise.

Two books inspired me, and I am in debt to their authors: *The Wilding* by Benjamin Percy and *After Visiting Friends* by Michael

Hainey. Reading Percy's novel felt like experiencing the three generations of my family that will never meet, like taking my children on the hunting trip with my father and me that has become mythic in my imagination. Michael Hainey writes, in his memoir, "All my life, I've felt the story I was told about how my father died did not add up." Hearing him say that gave me permission to say it too.

Enormous thanks to the faculty at the Pacific University MFA program (especially Jack Driscoll, Pam Houston, Benjamin Percy, and Debra Gwartney). A giant thank you to Nick Flynn and the Tin House Summer Workshop too. Pam Houston recognized I was a nonfiction writer before I did, Debra Gwartney taught me that I couldn't write a memoir without putting myself in it, and Nick Flynn showed me how to channel my inner poet.

Huge shout-out to Tabitha Blankenbiller, who invited me to join her memoir critique group. Thank you to the other members too, who offered helpful suggestions and essential moral support: Stephanie Bane, Katie Martin, Tiffany Hauck, Crystal Bevers, and Charlotte O'Brien. Thank you to Holly Lorincz and Kat Setzer for helping make this book better. Thanks to Artis Henderson, Lori Horvitz, Jesse Lee Kercheval, Alexandria Marzano-Lesnevich, Hope Mills Voelker, Kristen-Paige Madonia Gordon, and Jody Hesler for encouragement and understanding.

Thank you to Deborah Reed for guidance and friendship. Thank you to Leigh Camacho Rourks, my "writing partner." At our MFA graduation, the faculty advised us all to pair off into writing partnerships so we could e-mail every day and keep each other accountable. Leigh has done this for me, for years, and so much more.

I'd like to thank the WriterHouse staff, especially Rachel Unkefer, Sibley Johns, and Lisa Ellison, as well as the students I've been privileged to teach, who have taught me more than I've taught them.

Finally, of course, I want to acknowledge the generous love and support of my family. Thank you to my brother, mother, aunt, and uncle for sharing their memories. Thank you to my husband, daughter, and son, for allowing me to write about them with such candor. Thank you to my mother- and father-in-law and my other aunts and uncles too. It can't be easy having a memoirist in the family.

And to James: I still feel lucky you chose me. You're the best life partner a writer could ask for, and you give me joy.

About the Author

Sharon Harrigan's essays and short fiction have appeared in *The New York Times*, *Virginia Quarterly Review*, and *Narrative*. She received the Joyce Horton Johnson Award from Key West Literary Seminar and the Kinder Award from *Pleaides*, as well as fellowships from the Virginia Center for the Creative Arts and Hambidge. Educated at Barnard College, Columbia University (BA), and Pacific University (MFA), she teaches memoir writers at WriterHouse, a nonprofit writing center in Charlottesville, Virginia, where she lives with her husband and children.

Photo courtesy of Sarah Cramer. Used by permission.